Talking Tombstones

and Other Tales

of the Media Age

Talking Tombstones

and Other Tales

of the Media Age

Gary Gumpert

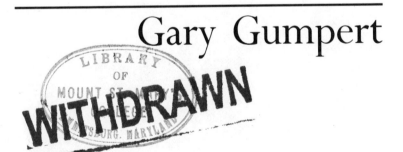

New York • Oxford
Oxford University Press • 1987

Oxford University Press

Oxford   New York   Toronto
Delhi   Bombay   Calcutta   Madras   Karachi
Petaling Jaya   Singapore   Hong Kong   Tokyo
Nairobi   Dar es Salaam   Cape Town
Melbourne   Auckland
and associated companies in
Beirut   Berlin   Ibadan   Nicosia

Published by Oxford University Press, Inc.,
200 Madison Avenue, New York, New York 10016

Library of Congress Cataloging-in-Publication Data

Gumpert, Gary.
  Talking tombstones and other tales of the media age.

  Bibliography: p.
  Includes index.
  1. Mass media—Moral and ethical aspects.   2. Mass media—Technological innovations.   3. Mass media—
Social aspects.   I. Title.
P94.G86   1987   302.2′34   86-28652
ISBN 0-19-503811-8 (alk. paper)

10 9 8 7 6 5 4 3 2 1
Printed in the United States of America
on acid-free paper.

Contents

Talking Tombstones

and Other Tales

of the Media Age

The Talking Tombstone, or Introduction to a Theme

In a frank imaginary conversation social satirist Russell Baker informed the late Henry James of the technical innovations of the 1980's through a "time-dissolving international punch-button code" telephone call.

> So I told him about the miracles of technology. I had plenty to do. By flipping a switch I could condition the air. Twisting a dial allowed me to watch grown men playing boys' games thousands of miles away. Activating my computer, I could obtain the reading on my bank balance. Adjusting my video screen, I could play a game with little electronic pictures while headphones, clamped to my ears, pumped music directly into my skull. With miraculous pills I could deaden my senses or achieve visions and frenzies—.
>
> `He interrupted. "But what do you do there?" He repeated, "Don't you have anything to do?"[1]

Baker's practical-minded scepticism indicates a disparity between the values of the past and the accomplishments of modernity. But suppose it were possible to communicate with the past, would that possibility alter the way we live in the present and think of the future? The idea

An especially haunting sense of tragedy emanates from this tomb-stone in Père-Lachaise Cemetery in Paris. Does he know that he poses for immortality and his own tombstone?

of telephoning George Washington or Charles Darwin is amusing and educational. With whom would you want to talk, and what meaningful questions would you ask? Reverse this hypothetical situation and accept the improbability of being able to communicate out of the past with the future, what would you want to reveal to your descendants? You can do this today if you buy a "talking tombstone".

Wandering through a cemetery—through the neat and well-ordered arrangement of paths and stones, of real and artificial flowers—who has not at some time felt something indescribable, something beyond the macabre or the mystical? Perhaps a shudder is triggered by the silent monolithic stones. Names and dates are hardly enough to provide any sense of the body buried beneath the tombstone. What is so compelling about the short epitaphs? In some European cemeteries photographs have been affixed to the tombstones, yet the photograph of a proud young Frenchman posing in his splendid army uniform and the inscription telling that he was killed in the Great War does not satisfy curiosity and imagination. "Who are you?" "What did you feel about the world in which you lived?" "What do you remember about your past?"

"Here lies John Doe / To hear his tale / Push button below." This rhyme introduced a story appearing in a 1977 issue of *People* magazine announcing an invention by John Dilks, a computer engineer with the Western Electric Company in New Jersey, who established a company to help the deceased and the survivors communicate. John Dilks and associates have come up with "imitations of immortality."

> A solar-powered headstone containing a recording device (for epitaph or words of admonition) and a video display screen on which can be beamed a biographical account, a genealogy and a computerized photograph. What's more, Dilks' Creative Tombstone, Inc., could add such options as sensors to tell when a visitor approaches or the grass needs watering, a nozzle to spray incense and a mechanized arm that emerges to trim the grass. The price is $39,500 for a vandal-proof headstone covered by bulletproof glass. . . .
>
> Dilks is already making sure no man will write his epitaph. He is designing a headstone with info about his wife, Sherry, and their four kids and some advice "for my great-great-great-great-grandchildren." It may not be worth waiting that long. The message is, "Do what's right, come what may." [2]

Most people have imagined what others would say about them after their deaths, and now there is a way to talk back with an interactive audiovisual computerized legacy. How many of us can escape from looking at the collection of photographs which constitute the family album? Someone is caught in a moment of time, and suddenly we have a fragment of understanding about the person and a sense of consanguinity with the shadowy past locked in the photograph. How much more vivid the legacy becomes as other sense modalities—more media—are used to preserve the past and to animate it in the present. The frozen glance of the camera eye is animated by the later technology: motion picture, video tape, audio tape, and video disc. Words inscribed on paper can be kept in an oral form by preserving an utterance on audio tape. The recording could even be turned on by a voice-activated sensor rather than a touch mechanism. The technological wizardry of the computer provides for the storage and retrieval of a series of bons mots and images which could be programmed to simulate individual idiosyncratic interaction. Responses can be imagined for any future inquiry.

Assume for the moment that the talking tombstone became economically feasible and was available to anyone who wished to leave a multimedia sepulcher as a last earthly statement. Who would refuse to leave to the future the insights and words of wisdom gathered over a lifetime? At what point in a person's life would the process of preparing this testimony begin? What family would not plead with its elderly to prepare a message before the day of departure? Is the idea farfetched? Can you imagine a contemporary family without photographs to document the children's growth? Yet, who before the nineteenth century could have imagined the impact of the photograph upon the average individual and family? Who now could resist the urge to find out what visions and messages were locked in the computerized gravestone? The cemetery is transformed into a Disneyland filled with countless treasure hunts.

It is not difficult to imagine such a perpetual testament's becoming commonplace. Of course, one can also imagine a power failure eliminating the entire sepulchral heritage, but computer memory need not be erased by power failure—at least a short one.

If it were a normal and accepted procedure, how would that technological tour de force affect attitudes toward life and death? It would have to leave some mark on the way people cope with those elements over which they have absolutely no power: birth is irreversible and death is inevitable—at least for the time being. Every medium has influenced our attitudes toward death and altered how we value posterity. From the moment when a human being discovered a means to leave a record of the present by preserving images for the future, the nature of genealogical relationships was changed forever.

There must pass through every writer's mind, perhaps just for a fleeting moment, the notion of eradicating time and space, the inconveniences that separate the conception and transmission of an idea. The living book, one in which the author and the reader converse, will some day be a reality of everyday life. In the meantime, *Talking Tombstones* takes on a more traditional form—a tradition molded by previous developments in technology and a particular bias for the printed tome.

Talking Tombstones makes a number of assumptions about our relationship to media technology. We as individuals are *not* in control of the technological environment in which we find ourselves. *Every generation inherits a particular media structure.* While each of us might seek to alter specific circumstances or influence social patterns, the individual inherits a legacy of technology. Those born into the age of radio are different from those born into a world where no electronic communication existed. Those who have never lived without a consciousness that includes television reception in the home have a different perspective from the generation that still remembers the miraculous introduction of those tiny black and white moving pictures viewed through a built-in magnifying device.

It is obvious, but nevertheless the statement needs to be made: *no technological phenomenon can be reversed.* It is impossible to dis-invent the telephone or the radio once it has been introduced into the fabric and consciousness of society. The concept of recording sound and images on some substance which makes it permanent and retrievable can not retrogress. You can't go backward, only forward, in the world of technology. Just as, however, a particular technology evolves into a higher or more developed form, other forms of media technology become obsolete. Obsolescence is the result of development, not stagnation. For example, the push button format of the telephone, an important feature in interconnecting it with a large number of interactive media, is based upon a transformation in which earlier features are becoming obsolete. Someday the telephone dial will be just another antique.

There has evolved in Western culture a growing dependency upon media of communication which is, to a great extent, often denied or overlooked. We have become addicted to the conveniences and services of media without an awareness that they are such an integral and important part of our culture. The radio is a device which serves us in many ways and allows us to select among all sorts of programs. What would you do without a radio? Would you be a different person? Think of that reliable companion found in almost every room in the home (only strange people don't have radios in their cars), which can be turned on and off, the content changed by simply pushing the button or twisting the knob, carried about wherever you are. What's a beach or bedroom without radio? The matter of dependency is a difficult issue to face, because that technological bond implies a loss of control and of independence. It is not a matter of judgment, but a statement of fact—*we are a media-dependent culture.* What media could be considered merely frivolous and nonessential to the business of living? Could you live without recorded music or the early morning weather report released by the clock radio alongside your bed? What media would you be willing to dispense with that you are using now? There are few in urban Western culture who are not media-dependent. Indeed, giving up any media accoutrements marks an individual as an eccentric. How many parents fought against the invasion of the television set into the home, while their children spent every spare moment over at the neighbor's watching the cartoons denied by Mommy and Daddy? We must accept, if we are living in a developed nation, that we are prisoners of media technology developed to improve the quality of life by eradicating the barriers to communication of time and space, barriers which were once accepted as inflexible physical limitations of the universe. Media are intrinsic to the twentieth century environment.

In the twentieth century the cornucopia of media has spilled out a plethora of innovations: the motion picture, radio, television, satellite communication, transistor radios, video disc recording, the tape recorder, digital audio and video recording, computer assisted instruction. Think of the rapidity of this change. It is likely that your great-grandparents lived without radio, that your grandparents remember a world without television, and that your parents were born into a world without stereo. Indeed, in your lifetime more innovations in media technology will be developed than all of the inventions introduced in all the many years preceding your existence.

Each person inherits the technological and cultural legacy of the age. Those born into the early age of photography swiftly internalized the concept of photographic images as metaphor and model. Can you think of the world without the subtle and pervasive influence on human consciousness of an invention which did not exist prior to 1839? One result of the internalization of photography into our cognitive processes is that we have learned to envisage each other in terms of the close-up. Media technology consists of more than gadgets that serve people; it alters the interactions and relationships of everyone in a society. This can be demonstrated by imagining the absence of any medium upon which we have become dependent. If, by some miraculous act, the telephone and our awareness of the telephonic act were suddenly to vanish, present urban civilization would be radically, if not totally, changed. The New York City power failure of the 1970s demonstrated our extraordinary reliance upon technology. Power failure is analogous to cultural stroke because it paralyzes the media apparatus which extends our sensory vision.

Unlikely communication possibilities have been accepted and transformed into expected probabilities. Consider the intimacy of a long distance phone call between San Francisco and Boston. The two cities remain the same distance apart today as they have always been, but the telephone permits instantaneous audio communication between the two locations. When someone can be intimate with you and yet be physically so far away, the concept of the geographical universe is altered. But the point is that the connection of two people conversing, but separated by three thousand miles, is no longer considered improbable or unusual. Auditory and visual images can transcend time and space. Before electronic media who would have thought it possible to place voices in a small box and summon them back whenever it was so desired? The thought of capturing images of people and storing them indefinitely would once have been considered bizarre, but the camera does precisely that. Each of us assumes the conventionality of media experiences previously considered unconventional. None of us really has to adapt to conditions which are assumed to be part of normal living. We have adapted to the long-term effects of technology, particularly media technology, which have amassed over the last several centuries.

Each medium of communication leaves its mark by altering our institutions and personal attitudes and values. In Victor Hugo's *Hunchback of Notre-Dame* the character of the archdeacon hyperbolically states that "the book will kill the church."

> Omitting the detailing of a thousand proofs, and thousand objections to what has been said, we may sum the matter up as follows: That architecture, up to the fifteenth century, was the chief register of humanity; that during this interval, no thought of any complexity appeared in the world that was not built as every religious commandment has its monument; that human nature, in short, had not thought of importance that it did not write in stone. And why? because every idea, whether religious or philosophic, is concerned in being perpetuated. The idea that has stirred the emotions of one generation desires to affect others, and to leave its trace behind. . . .
>
> In the fifteenth century, everything underwent a change. Humanity discovered a means of perpetuating thought more lasting and durable than architecture, and even simpler and easier. Architecture was dethroned. To the stone letters of Orpheus are to succeed Gutenberg's letters of lead.
>
> *The book will destroy the building.*[3]

Both institution and individual are subject to the revolutionary effects of technological change.

Often technical innovation will be small and unspectacular. Installing radios in automobiles was a small step and yet it had enormous effects upon American culture. There is a connection to be found in the building of interstate highways, the car radio, and long distance driving. The mobile society is accompanied by the guiding beacons of local radio stations.

Would you consider the development of the 45 rpm record an important technological contribution? RCA's attempt to merchandize a new record player for 45s was an economic failure, but the records which were to be played solely on it remained a format that allowed for the manufacture of relatively cheap unbreakable recordings. The "45" can be linked to the emergence of "rock 'n' roll" as a cultural force as recordings were made available for the adolescent and teenage market place. The "45" was the counterpart of the paperback book—small, easily disposable, and relatively cheap.

Out of one person's science fiction emerges another's reality. Who hasn't dreamed of telepathic communication? Perhaps the implant of a tiny communications device will one day allow us to automatically transfer thoughts without recourse to any medium except cognitive intention. Is teleportation merely a product of human fantasy? Would you be willing to categorically deny the possibility that human bodies can be transported from one space to another and reconstituted? On a less grandiose scale, is the transmission of smell viable? If sound and images can be electronically disseminated, why not smell—for better or for worse? Cloning is a unique communication possibility—what a way to perpetuate one's heritage! In short, each future generation will have some unique communication medium to shape its environment. Whether we have infinite capacity to handle the increasing number of communication innovations is another matter, but the drive of invention is ceaseless.

So many media innovations have crowded into the twentieth century that understanding media's effect is difficult. The rate of change and the need for adaptation which is demanded by innovation make it even more difficult. There is a sense of social turbulence, of a lack of synchrony, of a gap which separates people, primarily on the basis of age. The generation gap so frequently mentioned a decade ago referred to different attitudes and values perceived among parents and their offspring. A generation is technically a thirty-year period, but today the gap is narrower than a generation. There is now an elusive, qualitative difference that characterizes each decade, but the attempt to articulate those specific differences is an exercise in frustration. Such qualitative dissimilarities indicate the cultural obsolescence of perspectives, and media are one of many forces that reshape experience and world view. The Spanish philosopher Julian Marias has commented on this sense of dislocation which is so difficult to articulate.

> We must seek the present, "the now," that eludes us. In referring to the present, we often say "these days" or "our time." But just whose time do we mean? When an old man says "in my day" he is referring not to the present in which he actually lives and speaks but to some past time. To which portion of the past does he feel he belongs? With what zone of his life does it coincide? When an old person speaks of "my time," meaning some past period, he seems to reveal that he lives in the present as an exile or an alien. Are not our lives formed by the very subtle essence of a certain period?[4]

The essence of "my time" and "your time," while vaguely distinct, is nevertheless closer in years than ever before. Media technology disconnects us from our immediate past and future and atomizes people of disparate ages caught in a flux of technological acceleration.

The sociologist Melvin L. DeFleur has stated that "values are enduring beliefs that define certain modes of conduct or states of existence as personally and socially preferable."[5] In *The Nature of Human Values* Milton Rokeach provides a more elaborate explanation:

> To say that a person has a value is to say the he has an enduring prescriptive or proscriptive belief that a specific mode of behavior or end-state of existence is preferred to an oppositive mode of behavior or end-state. This belief transcends attitudes toward objects and toward situations; it is a standard that guides and determines action, attitudes toward objects and situations, ideology, presentation of self to others, evaluations, judgments, justification, comparisons of self with others, and attempts to influence others.[6]

Values are enduring and more constant than attitudes. Attitudes involve a set of opinions about a specific situation. Our attitudes emerge out of our underlying beliefs and values. We have attitudes toward objects, things, and symbols. Values are less mercurial, but they do change: both in their hierarchical relations with each other and independently. According to Rokeach some values are "terminal" and refer to idealized ends one would wish to reach or attain (equality, freedom, happiness) and some are "instrumental," which define the preferred patterns of behavior for working toward those ends (honesty, cleanliness, responsibility). Some values are testable, some are relative, and others are nondebatable. There would be little debate over terminal values because they are recognized as ends that are achieved, partially achieved, or not achieved at all. On the other hand, honesty, trust, and courage, while agreed upon as ideals, are often not acted upon. Most mortals fall short of the ideal, but the guiding belief in honesty lurks in the background—even for those who don't practice it. There is a third set of values which, while consisting of ideals or standards, are judged on a relative basis. Intelligence, comfort, cleanliness, and imagination are judged comparatively: Some people are more imaginative than others, some require less comfort than others. We judge and compare.

Although values tend to endure, they are not static beliefs which remain constant. They are reinforced, de-emphasized, altered, and redefined by the totality of one's experience. In each age values shift in priority. In a culture that relies less on the media, values are taught primarily through traditional relationships and associations. The family, the school, and the church are the teachers and touchstones of attitudes, beliefs, and values. But with the growth and development of media we have become increasingly dependent upon media for the support and education that more traditional institutions previously provided. It has been estimated that the average home has one or more television sets turned on for over five and a half hours a day. Add to that figure the number of hours spent listening to the radio, playing records, reading (newspapers, magazines, comic books, and books), and the total figure represents a great deal of time spent in media encounters instead of in interpersonal contacts. And some of that personal interaction is itself mediated by the telephone. A third of our waking hours are spent with media, and this does not include the use of media at work or in school. That force must be considered of great importance.

A great deal has been said and written about the effects of the mass media upon the individual and the family. Countless writers have examined the media world, and many social scientists are investigating how the public utilizes the media, the effect media has upon children, how the mass media influences politics. There are many questions that need to be asked about why individuals turn to the content of the mass media, but it is also important to examine the intrinsic characteristics that define each medium and that in turn affect values and attitudes. But to restrict such a focus to *only* the mass media, as opposed to all media, would be a mistake. It is necessary to distinguish between the two, because "mass media" represents the institutionalization of certain media and refers to the use of media for a large section of the public. However, a "medium" of communication is merely the means or instrument by which information is replicated and/or disseminated. The term "media," therefore, refers to a technology and a system which can be utilized for point-to-point communication, dissemination of material or interaction between groups of people, and mass communication. No medium is intrinsically a "mass medium."

Media preserve and transform values. For example, by virtue of its ability to link people in different places with a sound channel, the telephone potentially encourages spatial friendship by aurally connecting people who are separated by space. Relationships are therefore not limited to immediate face-to-face interaction or to letters. In this case what is valued in a friendship shifts a degree because of the basic capability of a medium. The opportunity to talk to other people without being in their presence is cherished as privacy increasingly is prized. In other words, it is sometimes important *not* to be close to someone and yet to be able to communicate fairly spontaneously. In a similar way, the capacity of the camera to isolate and fragment images of the past alters our relationship with time. Independence and memory are intertwined as we experience life knowing that the portable past is available to the present and future through the photograph. The link between past and present preoccupies many people whose identity is revealed and preserved by the camera's eye and the family album.

Talking Tombstones looks at the artifacts of media technology which emerged out of the inventiveness, imagination, and needs of the human being to transcend limitations to communication. There is an innate drive to spread the images and sounds of the mind over time and space, to make the impossible possible, the improbable commonplace. That creative and inventive urge remains constant, but the effects of our inquisitive nature reverberate far beyond the moment of inspiration and invention. The artifact speaks and we all listen. The inventions and technology of communication reach all and penetrate the consciousness of individual and culture. These inventions are living monuments which continue to shape our nature and vision.

Samuel Morse's invention of the telegraph in 1844 was the first invention to provide instantaneous communication of information through space. Contemplate the enormity of that feat before our contemporary communications glut. Think about how extraordinary the possibility of sending and receiving messages electronically over distance was. Henry David Thoreau's reaction was less than embracing when in *Walden* he said, "We are in great haste to construct a magnetic telegraph from Maine to Texas, but Maine and Texas, it may be, have nothing important to communicate . . . as if the main object were to talk fast and not to talk sensibly." What Thoreau failed to observe is that the distance between Maine and Texas would irrevocably shrink.

One

The Fake Horses
of San Marco

Pollution has begun to devastate the regal horses of San Marco in Venice. The acid rains have endangered these bronze creatures, and the authorities have had to take the drastic expensive action of removing them, preserving them in a pollution-free environment and, over a period of time, replacing the originals with replicas. The reproductions are exact replicas of the horses—*to every last detail.* The average person would not be able to distinguish between the original bronze figures and the substitutes.

How to preserve art is not in question, but our reaction to the proxy horses does raise some provocative issues about attitudes toward a work of art. Is the artistic experience, one's appreciation of the noble horses, changed in any way by the knowledge that an exact substitute is before us? How are we affected by the realization that we are not viewing the original work, but a facsimile? What makes us value those proud horses?

Assume that you are not aware that any of the original horses have been removed. Your experience is shaped by two sets of factors. The

Only careful perusal reveals the date of the replicas of the horses of San Marcos. Small inscriptions inform the curious visitor who has climbed up to inspect the horses carefully that the horses on view from the Piazza were made in the 1970's. The originals, protected from the pollution of Venice, are kept in a room a few feet away.

first set stems from that immediate confrontation between you and the horses. Are they beautiful, handsome, ugly? Are they startling, sad, raging, and inspiring? The senses feel the elements that were formed by the creator, but the personality of the artist is submerged as we actively participate in the aesthetic experience of that moment. The second set of reactions involves the historical context of the art object, and here the matter of antiquity comes to the foreground. How old are the horses? What were the circumstances of their creation? How did they get to Venice? The artist's life becomes a matter of interest to the viewer, and the material or financial worth of the four horses is enhanced by the historical context. Actually, the date and place of origin of the horses are unknown, although they are attributed to either a Greek or a Roman artist. It is known that the horses of San Marco were transported to Venice in 1204 as war booty after the conquest of Constantinople by the Crusaders and the Doge Enrico Dandolo. In the historical sense, the monetary value of the horses is influenced by their dramatic heritage. They are priceless because of their age and beauty. The drastic action of creating replicas was done from the desire to preserve the original horses. Their value would be far less if they had been designed and cast in 1986. Awareness of the facsimile weakens the bond between the historical heritage and the appreciator. That is, if you know that you are not viewing the original, then the historical context cannot be a determinant of value. Several years ago one of the horses toured a number of museums around the world. Would your experience of that art object have been altered if it had been revealed that the exhibited horse was a fake?

The horses are unique because of a special vision, a peculiar creative force manifested in their creation. They are unique because of the specific relationship between spectator and the work of art which is limited to a time and a place—unless one sees a copy of the horses, or the originals are taken out of their setting from the facade of the Basilica of San Marco, or photographs of the horses are seen. One can argue the relevance of context in the appreciation of art. Certainly, the sense of place which surrounds the four horses adds to their grandeur, but it is quite possible to appreciate, to admire the work, out of its traditional environment.

People from all over the world come to see the marvelous Horses of San Marco. They travel at great expense and with much ado. If the horses, which are deteriorating, can only be saved by replacing them with exact replicas—which cannot be distinguished from the original (except by trained observers), why can't multiple "horses" be produced and copies distributed to a number of museums around the world, so that more people could enjoy and marvel at their grace and beauty? Multiple copies of the horses can be created. Why not make a few more? Why does anyone have to be told the facts surrounding their manufacture? The Horses of San Marco can come to the people.

Perhaps the Venetian authorities ought to inform spectators that they are in the presence of copies and therefore should mitigate their aesthetic passions. But such an act of "truth in art" would be distracting and demoralizing. Those spectators who view the horses from the piazza are not aware of the substitutions. Those who climb up to inspect the horses more closely will find a small plaque or inscription indicating the date of manufacture of each horse. Ironically, most people are still enjoying the spectacle of the Horses of San Marco out of ignorance, because they have not been informed that they are actually looking at unusually well-crafted copies.

Two people approach the Horse of San Marco displayed at the Metropolitan Museum of Art in New York. (In case you are wondering, museum authorities have confirmed that the exhibited horse was *authentic.*) For all except the devoted art expert, authenticity is verified by the label or plaque placed near the object by the museum curator. Just for the sake of argument, however, assume that the horse displayed at the 1979 Metropolitan Museum exhibit was *not* authentic. Two individuals stand before the horse. One believes that she is looking at the original authentic horse, the other is aware that the object is a facsimile. The former enjoys the moment out of ignorance, the latter's concern over authenticity influences what might have been a moment of emotional insight or elevation.

What is apparent is the confusion that exists between the aesthetic experience and the historical one, between the value of scarcity and the essence of that moment of artistic confrontation. Traditionally it has been assumed that a work of an artist would be unique and limited. One Mona Lisa was created by Da Vinci and our emotional response to that visual enigma is theoretically limited to the particular work which hangs in a specific location at the Louvre in Paris. Nevertheless, each of us became aware of *the* Mona Lisa, or any other famous work of art, before ever coming face to face with the specific work. Each of us has seen photographs and reproductions of the masterpiece. But there is only one true Da Vinci rendering of *the* Mona Lisa!

While Da Vinci used the medium of paint and canvas to express his vision, the contemporary artist has new media available which do not restrict him or her to a one-to-one relationship of created object and viewer. The photographer has no limitations upon the number of prints that can be created from a negative except those that time and energy impose. The graphic arts are characterized by the ability inherent in the media to create multiple copies of a particular work. Indeed the artist deliberately restricts the number of prints by signing and numbering a limited edition. The restraint is artificial and is based upon art economics, not aesthetics.

In *The Work of Art in the Age of Mechanical Reproduction,* Walter Benjamin points out that works of art have always been "reproducible," that "artifacts could always be imitated,"[1] but mechanical reproductions of a work of art represent a new development. There was a time when all works were original, or at least were restricted by the artist's ability to duplicate that very same work. To duplicate a work involves repeating the identical process of technical creation that the artist initially had to pursue, although each subsequent copy would differ slightly because of infinite factors which come into play as the work is created. A drawing can be traced, a painting copied, the bust sculptured once again. Variation is unavoidable, and each copy has a facet of originality as each becomes a variation on a theme. Each rendering is unique.

Certain artistic means depend upon the technology of duplication. As Benjamin says, "with the woodcut graphic art becomes mechanically reproducible for the first time, long before script became reproducible by print."[2] Multiple etchings can be produced from a plate. Many copies can be produced through lithography. Numerous casts can be made from an original sculpture.

The distribution of the artifact is an inherent property of certain media. The printing of *one* book, while possible and sometimes even arranged, would certainly seem to be a strange and impractical use of the printing press. Why would the artist create just one print from an etching when the very plates exist for the production of further copies? At the same time, it would seem bizarre, to say the least, if the great Da Vinci dedicated his life to producing identical multiple copies of the Mona Lisa—painting one canvas after the other seeking to eliminate as many variations as possible. Identical renderings of a theme are alien to a medium such as oil painting. The goal and dream of the artist is to create that one masterpiece, the one work which will endure. Each work, therefore, is eccentric as it varies with each rendering.

Some media stress availability through multiplicity. Photography, for example, democratizes certain aspects of artistic vision because it is possible to reproduce its images and to distribute unlimited copies to all. Although there was a time when the absence of a negative made exact duplications an impossibility, the presence of the negative, in large part, defines the medium of photography. The reproductive nature of the photographic medium serves two broad functions: to create and communicate a peculiar visual insight into some aspect of the world— the artistic and rhetorical dimension of the medium—and to disseminate other media by producing facsimiles. The camera can reproduce an image of whatever is placed in front of the lens. A photograph of a piece of sculpture involves the fusion of two media: photography and sculpture. The photograph is a two-dimensional representation of a three-dimensional object (except when a two-dimensional object is being photographed). In most cases the object has been reduced in size, or perhaps a detail has been magnified.

Normally, the representation of a work is not confused with the original creation. However, a photocopy of a lithograph or a drawing can be almost indistinguishable from the original and only careful perusal would reveal the original from the copy. The matter of the relationship of an "original" to a "copy" of that original is relevant to this discussion because attitudes toward those terms are founded in the *technology which facilitates duplication.* Most people place a higher value on the original than on a copy of it. Is the presumption correct? Given the choice, would anyone ever select the copy? The bias is firmly implanted. Would you not prefer the Pierre Cardin slacks to an imitation made of equally good material? The only compelling reason not to would be economic. The relative cheapness of the copy could affect the decision. However, given the choice between the limited first edition of a book or an etching, as opposed to exact duplicates of that volume or print, the original is chosen.

Your reactions to the following hypothetical situation might demonstrate how the technology of duplication affects our value of scarcity. A famous author responds to your recent letter of praise with a personal handwritten thank-you note. Of course, you are overwhelmed, since the response is a treasured direct communication between you and that famous person. A personal relationship has been established where previously only one-sided artistic respect had existed. You have collected a personal memento of greatness. This is a rare letter to be prized and in order to protect the letter you rush to the best Xerox machine available and make four copies in case the original is ever lost. You carefully put the set of papers away until several weeks later, when another devotee of the author is visiting you, the urge to display the coveted letter cannot be resisted. Out come the five sheets of paper from their secure cache and you begin to feel a bit insecure. The products of this photocopy machine are excellent—too excellent. Which of the five sheets of paper is the original? They all look identical and only microscopic examination would tell the original from the copies.

The insecurity begins to mount into a frantic feeling edging on panic. Suddenly it becomes quite important to show your friend the true 100 percent original personal note and not the copy of the true 100 percent original personal note. You had even thought of giving a copy to your friend, but that's impossible now since you might be giving away the original.

How would you react? Would you give away one of the letters knowing that the chances were one out of five that you would be giving away the original? A number of reactions are possible. First, it doesn't matter, since the value exists in what is being communicated and not in the piece of paper itself. The sentiments are important, not the package they came in. This is the rational, functional approach which deemphasizes both the aesthetic dimension and the potential monetary value of the communique. Such crass commercial thoughts had not occurred to you? Certainly for many people the autographed letter becomes a potentially valuable financial asset, but in that case the personal nature of the letter would be relatively unimportant since the fact that it comes from a celebrity is far more important than the relationship between the writer and the recipient of the letter.

A second reaction to the dilemma is to assert categorically that a solution to the problem must be found because the impact of the letter only exists in the original piece of paper. Why? In this case the need to find the authentic original assumes manic proportions that cannot be explained rationally.

What is the source of this strong attachment to the letter? For those who are faithful to the cult of originality, it has do with a qualitative essence which is absent in the copy. The "genuine" version includes the essence, the spirit, of the communicator who has touched the paper, whose pen deftly and carefully inscribed those very words which are being read. In that sense, the letter is an intimate part of the author extended to an acquaintance. The author never touched the copy—the photocopy is the exact non-essence facsimile. The strongest argument for the adoration of the original is the sense of intimate contact, perhaps a figment of the imagination or the expression of a deep need to touch fame or power, which is somehow satisfied by a simple symbolic act. That intimate contact is almost physical in nature, in the sense that the letter transmits some residual touch, the sweat or the moment, the invisible fingerprint, of the communicator. It seems far-fetched, but what binds us to the written remnants of the past?

In a world where once only "originals" existed, the exact duplicate has become commonplace. The capability to repeat the singular act also creates some problems. The linking of photomechanical reproduction techniques with the medium of graphic prints has resulted in confusion over what is meant by the term "original." In recent years the art collection world has confronted the rise of the "fake" print phenomenon. The situation became so serious that the Attorney General of New York City held a special hearing in 1980. Miro, Chagall, Calder, Dali, Rockwell, Sloan, and Wyeth are "among [the] artists whose works or signature is being forged or sold."[3] One solution the Attorney General's office suggests is that certificates be issued to the buyer which explain "how, when, and by whom the copies were made and the exact extent to which the artist was involved in the process."[4] It has become relatively easy to reproduce works of art, particularly prints and sculpture, which could be appreciated as if they were originals because of their excellent reproductive quality. The average untrained person would not be able to discern the original from the fake. An acceptable definition of the term "original" is elusive. For example, take the case of the blank Salvador Dali masterpieces.

> Salvador Dali had for years contracted with various publishers to sign blank sheets of lithograph paper which would then be used for reproduction of his work to be sold as Dali "originals." Thousands, perhaps hundred of thousands, of these signed sheets are known to exist; in 1974 French customs police stopped a truck on its way into Andorra loaded with 40,000 sheets. . . . Last year Dali signed a number of contracts with Paris dealer Gilbert Hamon, allowing Hamon the right to

make reproductions from color slides of Dali's paintings, which, in some cases, the artist would mark with a special stamp bearing his thumb-print.[5]

The ambiguity surrounding the definition of an "original print" has its source in the fact that printing is a reproductive medium.

Traditionally an original print is an image *intended* to be a print as distinct from a reproduction, which *exactly* duplicates a work that already exists in another form.[6]

Because a reproductive medium can be further linked to another reproductive medium—graphic printing and photography—the problem of definition becomes absurd, beyond the task of articulating unethical practices. The concern over fraudulent practices is based in the economics of the system. Receding into the background is the pleasure provided by media which allow the many to enjoy a work rather than restricting that opportunity to the few.

Media can be classified on the basis of their propensity of duplication. Particular media are defined partly by the means by which they reach the intended audience. Therefore, the aesthetic value of media whose intrinsic nature is to be duplicated cannot be evaluated or judged with a criterion of scarcity. In the case of photography, the negative provides the means for producing multiple copies of an image, and as long as that negative remains available and intact, limiting the number of printed copies is either the result of economic motives or the dwindling energy of the photographer.

If the relationship of the artist and the final product is of importance, the determination of the "genuine" product becomes even more ambiguous as the direct hand of the artist becomes optional in the long, complicated creative process which culminates in a photographic print. If you take a photograph and send it to a laboratory for development, enlargement, and finally printing, have you created the photographs which are produced? There are many variations of this process. You could do your own printing and work on every nuance of the image until you arrived at the acceptable and expressive print. At this point that print could be sent to a laboratory which would reshoot your final print, creating a new negative from which multiple copies (the number specified by the artist) could then be produced. Should you die, and your photographs remain in demand, the executors of the estate could have further copies of that photograph printed. Where and when does the spirit of the artist cease to infuse a particular work? When does the printed photograph include the qualitative essence of the photographer, that sense of physicality which distinguishes the original letter from the photocopy? Is the photograph printed by the laboratory an example of a non-essence facsimile, which while providing aesthetic pleasure nevertheless is missing some part of the artist's imprint? Walter Benjamin has stated that "the presence of the original is the prerequisite to the concept of authenticity."[7] In that sense, the matter of originality and the qualitative essence of the artist is very important.

If one can keep economic factors on the periphery for the moment, what indefinable quality is absent in the mass-produced photograph? What is absent is that sense of physical relationship which normally binds spectator and artist when replication and duplication is not a factor. It is to that element which Benjamin refers when he speaks of "aura."

> One might subsume the eliminated element in the term "aura" and go on to say: that which withers in the age of mechanical reproduction is the aura of the work of art. . . . One might generalize by saying: the technique of reproduction detaches the reproduced object from the domain of tradition. By making many reproductions it substitutes a plurality of copies from a unique existence.[8]

The electronic media of radio and television were initially characterized by the absence of a physical property such as a negative. The evanescent nature of these media provided part of their appeal. The permanent work of art, the physical object, did not exist. The temporal quality of radio and television broadcasting stressed the simultaneous dissemination of content as the characteristic trait. While the salient feature of the telegraph and the telephone has been point-to-point transmission, that of radio and television has been the wide distribution of the electronic signal (the term "broadcasting" is derived from the agricultural concept of "casting the seeds broadly"). Therefore, multiplicity of reception was built into the very medium. Limiting the availability of the program to the few does not increase the value of the aesthetic experience. Indeed, that experience does not depend upon the limitation or the de-quantification of the experience. While the electronic media's potential is linked to the dissemination of a signal to a widely distributed audience, the *aesthetic* value of the specific program is not linked to quantification. Whether two hundred, two thousand, or twenty million people watch *Mash, Dallas, Dynasty,* or *Cagney and Lacey* is irrelevant to the degree to which such programs are enjoyed by an individual viewer in the privacy of the home. However, for the business interest of the broadcasting industry, the number of people in the audience signals the survival or demise of a programming venture. For the individual viewer the reception of a broadcast is a matter of private consumption of a public experience. While the number of people who share the program at that very same moment is of no importance, each member of that audience probably assumes the existence of a simultaneously participating audience with that particular program at the same time.

As long as the traditional structure of broadcast dissemination remains as the model, scarcity is irrelevant to the audience's experience of a production. But as the dissemination pattern changes from a broadcast to a disc or cassette model, the attitude of the audience changes; programs are not disseminated electronically, but collected, and this adds value which, while extrinsic to the content of a program, is nonetheless a dimension which becomes important. The newer communication technologies have stimulated a shift in control: when to engage in the act of entertainment is placed at the individual's own discretion and convenience. The viewer decides when to watch a program, whereas formerly the broadcaster dictated the moment by scheduling the program at a specific time.

Broadcasters have used audio and videotape to alleviate scheduling problems and as a production technique, that is, to delay and/or transport programs and to edit the content. With the video cassette recorder and the video disc playback unit, programming can be either bought or rented. The video cassette unit also allows for off-the-air recording of broadcast signals. The possibility of buying, renting, or recording off-the-air alters the relationship and attitude between person and program. What had been a temporal experience is suddenly modified by the addition of an object which contains that experience. Each person can search for, gather, and possess desired programs. In addition, the entire aesthetic relationship between viewer and program is changed as the ephemeral one-time experience is replaced by the repeatable event. In some respects the performance is similar to reading a book, in which pace and page are controlled by the reader and not by the author.

The new media technology has transformed those temporal arts whose duration was only the time of performance into collectibles which can last for an indefinite time and which can be brought to life at will. The phonograph record, the audio tape recording, the video disc and cassette follow the same pattern as the book, magazine, and newspaper as they become a potential part of the personal library. The *limited edition* in electronic media form is a distinct possibility. Why produce many copies of the program, when *few* are more valuable? It is ironic that the *mass* media could potentially contribute to the concept of scarcity as a determinant of art value, but it is a distinct possibility either because of intentional limitations placed upon the production of a program or because of time and wear which depletes the original copies of programs produced. Even the mediocre work can become a financial asset as it is transformed from prosaic oblivion when it is rediscovered as a "Golden Oldie," an ancient curiosity! Imagine that fifty years from now you are in possession of *all* extant copies of *General Hospital*!

This is not a new phenomenon, as the value of old comic books, magazines, and various other memorabilia indicates. What is novel is the collection of audio/visual *performances* and that such gathering will be commonplace. Whereas, at one time, only symbolic representations of a performance existed in the form of scripts and scores, now the performance itself is reproducible. The collectible performance began with the phonograph record. While motion picture film was used to record performances, as well as being an artistic performance in its own right, it had not become a part of each home's entertainment, educational, and intellectual repository. It is only now as motion pictures are being stored on video cassettes that renting, borrowing, or buying a film has become commonplace.

The economic structure of the arts and media do influence what people read, listen to, and watch. While the number of people who watch *Dynasty* does not alter the dramatic value and structure of the television production, it is quite apparent that a commercial system of broadcasting (and perhaps even a noncommercial system) evaluates success by the percentage of the population a show serves. The commercial broadcaster uses the figure represented by "cost per thousand," the cost to the advertiser of delivering a message to one thousand people. The lower the CPM the greater the economic success of the media venture. The product in commercial broadcasting is an audience delivered to an advertiser by a radio or television station. The advertiser buys time with the tacit understanding, based upon surveys, demographics, and crystal-ball gazing, that a particular time and program will attract the right kind of audience, in size and *ability,* to purchase the advertiser's product. Failure is measured in two ways—in attracting too small an audience and in losing to a media competitor whose program attracts a greater share of the available audience at that specific time. Success is achieved through programming that attracts the largest possible audience for as long as possible, preferably for an entire afternoon or evening. The program is seen as a means to an end and not as an end in itself. This condition creates a creative environment in which artistic expression is generally subservient to the economic needs of the commercial broadcasting system. The costs are staggering and the profits can be dazzling. On November 21, 1980, eighty-three million people (53.3 percent of American households) watched the episode of *Dallas* that revealed the identity of the culprit who shot J.R.—the anti-hero of this evening soap opera. Seventy-six percent of all television sets were tuned to the station which broadcast the episode. The advertisers who sponsored the show paid from $150,000 to $250,000 for each of the thirty-second commercials played within the limits of that one hour, and they reaped the harvest of such an extraodinary exposure of their commercial message and product. The National Association of Broadcasters' Code recommends a maximum of nine minutes and thirty seconds of commercial time during a primetime hour of television. Eighteen thirty-second commercials aired during primetime, at the low $150,000 figure generate $2,700,000. In 1980 it cost $650,000 to produce a one-hour episode of *Dallas,* and the cost to CBS, the network which carried the show, would be somewhat higher, since the producer makes a profit. Such figures do not include profit accrued from rerunning the segment, syndication, and international distribution. The scope of investment is suggested by the fact that a large corporation such as the telephone company spent about eighteen million dollars in one year to buy time for approximately twenty commercials which were aired nationally.[9] In 1986 the principle remains the same, although the costs of production and airtime have skyrocketed.

The economics of the entertainment business dictate the need for profit, and therefore any product such as a television program, a record, or a motion picture must appeal to a wide audience. For this reason, the esoteric, the avant-garde, the insightful but disturbing, the difficult, the strange, and the experimental types of entertainment do not surface frequently. The broadcaster, who must accept the system or leave it, is forced to play the media crap game. Uniqueness is rejected in favor of the predictable. The familiar is preferred to the strange and the traditional outweighs the experimental. In short, formula-based programming is stressed because it is the safest means to ensure profit. The basic ingredients of the formula include broad based emotional appeals, fast development of ideas, action, stock or stereotypical characters who are quickly recognized, and noncontroversial material. The formula often works, although since not every show or series is a hit some element of chance still remains. The public is offered an appealing potpourri which succeeds in satisfying an extraordinary segment of the population. In *TV: The Most Popular Art,* Horace Newcomb agrees that television is "essentially a formulaic medium in terms of its entertainment."[10] John Cawelti's study of the Western genre is revealing about the nature of formula.

> A formula is a conventional system for structuring cultural products. It can be distinguished from invented structures, which are new ways of organizing works of art. Like the distinction between convention and invention, the distinction between formula and structure can be envisaged as a continuum between two poles; one pole is that of a completely conventional structure of conventions—an episode of the Lone Ranger or one of the Tarzan books comes close to this pole; the other end of the continuum is a completely original structure which orders inventions—*Finnegans Wake* is perhaps the ultimate example.[11]

FORMULA AND THE ARTS

The degree to which formula is applied is a matter of critical judgment. The mass arts are popular and there can be no doubt that they are *more* appealing to the majority of people than "high culture" or "fine art." They are popular because they meet the immediate needs of the audience for easily digested entertainment. *Dallas,* or *Dynasty,* or reruns of *I Love Lucy* satisfy a larger proportion of the population than *Hamlet* or *Hedda Gabler* can ever hope to approach. The mathematics of audience provides the evidence. If one theatre with a seating capacity of 2000 seats were to be completely filled 365 days a year, it would take 113 years to reach the number of persons that viewed that single episode of *Dallas* broadcast on November 21, 1980. It becomes tempting to expound the virtues of art and to decry the pagan appeals of mass culture. Certainly, a great deal of passion has been spent in condemning the Madison Avenue philistines for their crass commercialism . . . and success. An equal amount of fervor has been spent praising the guardians of high culture. The dwindling elitists claim that "television is chewing gum for the eyes." The popularists espouse the needs of the people and condemn the aristocratic cultural coterie that worships the chic. What is lost in the dialectic is the role of the medium itself in shaping our attitudes toward "experiencing art." (The term "art" is used in its broadest sense in this context.) The chasm which separates the factions has widened, and lost in the plethora of arguments is the realization that fine art is not a substitute for mass art or vice versa. Henry Pleasants writing about his love for jazz indicates the emotional nature of the fracas.

> One is accused immediately of equating commercial success with artistic quality, the implication being that everything conventionally classified as Popular is commercially successful, which it isn't, and that commercial success and artistic quality are mutually exclusive, which they aren't. One is accused of accepting the Hit Parade and the Top Forty as infallible arbiters of artistic achievement, although little of the music that we are talking about ever appears on either. One is accused finally, of committing our musical culture to the dictates of the jukebox and the disc jockeys, about which the jazz community has rarely been heard to utter friendly a word.
>
> Our common technique of counterattack consists in setting up the most advantageous juxtapositions. One contrasts the Hit Parade or the Top Forty with the St. Matthew Passion or the Ninth Symphony and returns in triumph to the ivory tower.[12]

The functional distinctions and virtues of the popular arts and high culture are seldom considered. The overriding implication is that the masses consume or enjoy a culture which differs significantly from that enjoyed either now or in the past by the elite members of society. The contention is that there is a difference in both the content and quality of the product, that when cultural objects are transmitted and diffused through the mass media they are affected by this very act of transmission, by their marketability, and by the size of the market that enjoys them. The elitist fear voiced by critic Dwight MacDonald is that mass culture will drive out high culture, and that when high culture is produced for the masses it is immediately corrupted.

Like nineteenth-century capitalism, Mass Culture is a dynamic, revolutionary force, breaking down the old barriers of class, tradition, taste, and dissolving all cultural distinctions. It mixes and scrambles everything together, producing what might be called homogenized culture, after another American achievement, the homogenization process that distributes the globules of cream evenly throughout the milk instead of allowing them to float separately on top. It thus destroys all values, since value judgments imply discrimination. Mass culture is very, very democratic: it absolutely refuses to discriminate against, or between, anything or anybody. All is grist to its mill, and all comes out finely ground indeed.[13]

The majority of Americans do not go to museums or the symphony unless forced to by social pressure. The majority do not care to read or attend a production of *King Lear* or to listen to *Wozzeck*. And yet . . . somewhere in the back of one's consciousness there exists a nagging feeling that one ought to be familiar with and enjoy the great works of the present and the past, that one is not a "complete" person without some familiarity with "the arts"! We feel a twinge of guilt as we watch *Barnaby Jones* or *The Match Game* instead of the "good stuff" on the public television channel.

The antagonistic relationship between high and mass culture is compounded by several other factors. The average person is exposed to a constant daily diet of mass culture (radio, television, recordings, newspapers, magazines, and myriad forms of advertising), while far less frequently coming into contact with the objects of high culture. Casual fine art is a contradiction, but spontaneous brushes with mass culture are part of its context. The alienation of the individual from high culture has been introduced, in part, by an educational system which says, "it's good for you and you will suffer through it," reducing what should be fascinating encounters to intellectual exercises which have no relevance to their victims.

The situation is further complicated by the confusion of functions. Whereas the function of mass culture is to divert, amuse, and fill the empty gaps in a long day, the function of high culture is to elevate, inspire, and to stimulate introspection. Alan Gowans in *The Unchanging Arts* makes the observation that in painting "every single new development . . . for at least fifty years back can be traced to a source in popular, applied or commercial art." He indicates that this trend can be found in all the arts and is a reversal of the previous hierarchical value system in which high culture was the impetus for developments in mass culture. "The low arts [Gowan's term for the "mass arts"] are still capable of creating new forms because they are still in touch with life. But fine art has become an organism having no perceptible interaction with its environment."[14]

CULTURAL SELF-PROTECTION

The alienation and gulf between mass and high culture is further increased by the "cultural self-protection" syndrome. No one seeks to deflate his or her own cultural ego by adopting a view that their daily artistic encounters are of less value than others, particularly if "the others" are seen as outside the majority of society. Even though high culture is seen as a "bore one is supposed to appreciate," that qualitative shadow is not allowed to cast a shadow of inferiority upon all that is excluded from the superior, or included in that which is daily enjoyed and satisfying (the matter of function is forgotten). Some individuals recognize the functional distinctions but nevertheless continue to look at the products of each cultural camp on the bases of acceptance or nonacceptance. Rock is bad, modern art is ridiculous, and ballet is dull. Failing to see that there is inferior high culture and poor mass culture, the devotees react in the rhetoric of self-defense. Quality becomes monopolized in the war of cultural self-protection. The elite maintain the rigid position that only the fine arts embrace quality. The nonelite maintain an equally inflexible position that quality is subjective and, ergo, "beauty exists in the eye of the beholder and what *we* like automatically has quality." In "The Decline of Quality" Barbara W. Tuchman argues against the "eye of the beholder" position. "Quality as a condition of excellence implying fine quality as distinct from poor quality" is not subjective.[15]

> If I come closer, however, and suggest that quality is inherent in, let us say, the stark, exquisite fiction of Jean Rhys but not in "Princess Daisy," in New England's white-steepled churches but not in Howard Johnson's orange-roofed eateries, in the film "Ninotchka" but not in "Star Wars," Fred Astaire but not in Johnny Carson, I shall be pelted with accusations of failure to understand that what was once considered quality has given way under a change of social values to appreciation of new qualities and new values; that the admirers of the ceramic dolls and trash fiction and plastic furniture and television shows with their idiotic laughter

find something in these objects and diversions that mean quality to *them*—in short, that quality is subjective. Yes, indeed, just as there are men who believe and loudly insist they are sober and who stumble and weave and pass out five minutes later. The judgment is subjective but the condition is not."[16]

The yardstick for commercial success in broadcasting is massive quantity. The quality of quantity is the commercial ideal because the number of individuals who receive, view, or hear a particular work is important and not the judgment of the work itself. Economic success is substituted for artistic achievement as the priorities shift. For the institutional persona of corporate mass culture (writers, publishers, financiers, directors, advertisers, and artists) a good program or film is one which succeeds in attracting a great number of people, or at least more than its competitors attract. The content is relatively insignificant; if test patterns were saleable, they would be sponsored. It makes sense for a business to make money, but the cult of numbers also subtly seduces the viewer. Again, Barbara Tuchman is quite precise:

> The criterion for the goods and services and arts that society produces is the pleasure and purchasing power of the greatest number, not the most discerning. Therein lies the history of non-Q [nonquality]. Arts and luxuries may still be directed to the few and most discerning, but when the dominant culture is mass-directed and the rewards in money and celebrity go with it, we have to consider whether popular appeal will become the governing criterion and gradually submerge all but isolated rocks of quality.
>   Will the tides of trash obey Gresham's law to the effect that bad money drives out good? . . . I do not know whether, according to our ever-flexible economists, Gresham's law remains valid, but as regards quality in culture, it has gloomy implications.[17]

THE UNCONSCIOUS COLLECTIVE

The devolution of quality is stimulated and encouraged by the stress on quantification. In the privacy of her home the viewer is aware that she is joined by the great number of other persons who in the privacy of their homes watch the same program. The "unconscious collective"—the stated awareness that the individual audience member is simultaneously and privately joined in the same media act or encounter—has been an important and influential force upon the viewing, reading, and listening habits of the audience. One of the implications of the simultaneous act is that if so many people are participating in the same media event, there must be a positive value in participating in that event. Not only does one not care to believe that one is participating in an unworthy media act, but to do it collectively seems unthinkable. The defended uncelebrated act becomes worthy. Therefore, "cultural self-protection" plus the "unconscious collective" pits the mass audience against the tyranny of the elitist minority. It is media's intrinsic capacity to disseminate to the many that has been interpreted as a sign of success, and commercial success has become confused with artistic quality. Quantity and quality have become correlatives. We have moved from one position, which maintains that scarcity breeds value, to one that proclaims acceptance and quantity as determinants of artistic value. Both positions are absurd since they are extrinsic to the phenomenon of experiencing the artistic event. There is no doubt that media which have wide and simultaneous distribution can be devoted to culture for masses as well as to mass culture. Equally, the products of mass culture can be delightful diversions and stimulating entertainment easily consumed by a public which wants and seeks that level of entertainment. And sometimes moments of great beauty and insight emerge which captivate even the audience of high culture. There is no question that mass entertainment will continue to thrive, because it plays an important role in providing gratification to the majority of an entire nation. What explains the worldwide appeal of the products of all forms of American mass culture: television, film, popular music, clothing, fast food, etc.? The charge of cultural imperialism is not a satisfactory answer! The American culture factory provides instant pleasure!

NEW MEDIA: QUALITY VERSUS QUANTITY

The economics of entertainment have furthered the confusion between quantity and quality. The patrons' stress on scarcity, because of economic value and snobbishness, is a self-imposed rejection of mass culture. Perhaps very few people still assert, "I wouldn't have a television set in my house" (a fashionable statement once proclaimed by a vocal minority), but the aura of disdain still persists in the halls of the cognoscenti. An intelligent person does not watch television unless there are extenuating circumstances. The pattern has remained constant: "as

each new medium comes into being, the intellectual shies away."[18]
Critic Gilbert Seldes indicates another reason for the ascendancy of
popular culture.

> The theory that the artist was rejected by Americans because he dis-
> closed the emptiness of their lives is only half true; the other half is
> that the artist had little to give Americans, little that was relevant to
> their time and situation in the world. "The American intelligentsia,"
> says Eric Bentley, "consists of people isolated from their communities."
> The isolation is partly self-exile.[19]

The self-exile included the self-excommunication from those media whose
primary raison d'être was to serve the majority of the people. The
control and qualitative criteria for entertainment shifted from the aristocratic elite to the democratized middle class as that audience continues to be alienated (at an increasing rate) from anything tainted with
classicism, the literary, the avant-garde, or the experimental. The de-
monopolization of entertainment results from the accession of the substance of the mass media by the majority. The media characterized by
replication and duplication, by their ability to quantify a creative moment, were rejected by the intellectual community. The value of that
creative endeavor existed outside the work itself and was influenced by
its availability to the public. The rule of inverse aesthetic value persists
and stipulates that the restriction of quantity will influence quality.

THE DELIVERY OF VALUE

There is some hope that as the structure of the mass media is altered
by video cassette recorders, communication satellites, and cable television, the same media used to produce formula programming will be
used to create more meaningful artistic experiences. While a number
of companies were optimistic that fine arts programming was feasible,
economics still guides and strangles most attempts to escape from the
trap of formula. In 1981 William S. Paley, then the chairman of the
board at CBS, began CBS Cable with the intention of producing high-
quality cultural programming. CBS Cable went out of business in 1982
after losing more than thirty million dollars. The same fate awaited the
Entertainment Channel with its BBC and Broadway productions.
TeleFrance USA gave up in September of 1982 in its attempt to present
French cultural programs.

The economics of numbers dictates "hyphenated culture"—artistic endeavors tempered by the reality of attracting a large enough audience for profit to be accrued by *all* the participants in the venture. Before the development of cable, the technical limitations of the electromagnetic spectrum helped to create a transmissional oligopoly which, along with the economic bases of the system, colored and influenced the nature of the material that would be created and transmitted. The result was the steady homogenization of culture and entertainment for a vast audience which demanded constant satiation. Cable permits the stratification of services, but only as long as the audiences are commensurate with economic investment. The "electronic salon" will always compete and be compared with the success of a national variety show. Cable allows for some modest compartmentalizing of culture in which the goal of quantity is temporarily shunted in favor of style and eloquence, but homogenization and formula have such great appeal that the seduction of numbers will threaten to overwhelm attempts at quality. The primary ingredient that is conspicuously absent—the essence of the expressive aesthetic act—is the hand of the creative artist.

The interaction between the creator of an aesthetic experience and the person who experiences it is ultimately directed by the vehicle or medium through which the experience is delivered. Perhaps it was assumed at some point in history that a particular created work was unique—that is, that no other object exactly like it existed anywhere else in the world, although some artists might have endeavored to produce fairly exact replicas. But even in such cases the issue of authenticity was never simple, because the economic value of that work was determined by a matter of definition. How exact was the replica? In that regard Umberto Eco distinguishes between a "double" and a "replica." Eco termed the duplicative replica the "double," while he defined the "replica" as a partial rendering of the original. But even that distinction is not always clear.

> According to this notion of double, it is commonly supposed that a painting is not truly duplicable. This is not completely true for, under given technical conditions, and using the same materials, one could theoretically establish a perfect double of the Mona Lisa by means of electronic scanners and of highly refined plotters.[20]

But there have been artists whose intent was to create the exact replica—the double. The research of Richard E. Stone, the Associate

Conservator at the Metropolitan Museum of Art in New York, revealed that as early as the fourteenth century the Italian sculptor Pier Jacopo Alari-Bonacolsi of Mantua, called Antico, produced "identical replicas" of his small bronzes with the intent of selling the works to his patrons.[21] What is significant is that a new technology of bronze casting altered the relationship between artist, object, and patron. That intimate bond has been further attenuated with each new technological innovation of artistic medium in which the hand of the artist was further removed from that moment in which the work is revealed to an audience. The moment of creation and time of experience, once contiguous, grew apart.

The technological de-monopolization of the arts requires a distinction between object and experience. The purist would probably adhere to the position that anyone who cannot distinguish between replica and original is not worth any artistic consideration. But that position is hardly defensible without universal mandatory art education for all. Within a range of replication, the aesthetic reactions stimulated by the original object and its doppelganger are equally valid and similar. The fake horses of San Marco and their authentic siblings standing silently in a chamber less than fifty feet away would evoke similar emotional responses if their environmental contexts were also similar. However, there is absolutely no question which of the two sets of horses is economically valuable, and the only reason for seeking to acquire the copies is to test them out on friendly victims who profess to be experts.

In the artistic worlds of radio, television, and film there are no fakes, only renditions removed from the aura of the artist and copies in which the physical quality present in the original begins to deteriorate as the audience experiences the artistic moment in subsequent generations of copies. There are no fakes in the mass arts, only moments of superficiality induced by the formula of each success and the search for masses of people who would constitute a large enough audience to permit the further production of pablum.

Two
The Ambiguity of Perception

It's a poor sort of memory that only works backwards.

Lewis Carroll

We depend upon concepts of time and space to function in and interpret reality. "Here and there," "now and then," "what was," and "what will be," are all percepts which guide us through the world. Without these operational frames fantasy could not be distinguished from reality, tomorrow would be today, and history would never have occurred. We assume that all "normal" individuals agree on basic definitions of time and space. For all there is an earlier and a later state, a past and a future. However, the world is changing and the development of modern media technology is altering the perceptual frames through which individuals function in their daily lives. The telephone allows a person to exist "here" and "there" simultaneously. "Yesterday" can be preserved through a photograph. Videotape permits "now" to be repeatable.

In most circumstances the frame of reality is quite evident. We believe we are aware of where and when we are. There is little chance for confusion—as long as the means of sensing the environment are not extended by mechanical/electronic media of communication. An awareness of time and space is implicit in communication. We know where we are when we communicate, and the medium utilized in the process provides clues for the indexing of that frame of time. The print in paper or book is read in the present, but written in the past. The grammatical structure of language further develops time and genre relationships between author and reader. The conventions are not generally articulated. On a simplistic level, if the author addresses you in the present tense, you play a game and pretend that the words are being spoken as you read them, knowing that this is not the case. The awareness of process and convention is central to the manipulation of time and space in communication.

From the perspective of the writer, fingers are in contact with typewriter keys in an attempt to convey thoughts. Writer and reader need to agree on a literary "now." "Now is momentary, fleeting, a transition between past and future, defined by what has happened and what will occur. We are bound to the present because of a belief that it, the present, is controllable, that the manipulable "now" determines the undetermined future. The author's "now" is transformed into the reader's "now" as these "past" thoughts are read. To complicate matters even more, the illusion of time is structured within fictional representations of reality.

There is value in knowing whether something perceived is a dynamic phenomenon "becoming," or something which has occurred and thus has already "become." And yet communication technology, especially television, has begun to blur and confuse one's relationship with mediated events. For example, what is meant in describing a program as being "live?" John J. O'Connor, television critic for the *New York Times* observed,

> The "live" label is still being marketed cleverly in today's programming. There are those shows that get the word "live" right into their titles: NBC's "Saturday Night Live," for instance, or public television's "Live From the Met" and "Live from Lincoln Center." Repeats of these programs are not live, needless to say, but the titles remain the same and most viewers seem to be completely unperturbed![1]

It is to be assumed that people recognize what is real and what is unreal or fabricated. Are they able, however, to tell the difference between a live program and one that has been recorded at a previous time? It is assumed that people can generally distinguish between signs and symbols, between an event and the construction of an event, but can they determine whether Jim McKay has been electronically inserted over the Olympic background or really is at a vantage point overlooking the arena? Human beings must classify events on the basis of medium, time, place, and genre if they are to order the incredible amount of sensory data which is processed each day. Is the perceived object or event transmitted via a medium? Is it occurring in the present or has it already happened? Where is it happening? What is the nature of the event: fiction or nonfiction, news or drama, an actuality or the reconstruction of an event?

A hypothetical situation will demonstrate the point. Walking down the street you suddenly witness a shattering automobile crash. The sound and sight produce an instant reaction: fear, shock, curiosity. But assume that a comparable event were witnessed on the television screen in your living room. It is conceivable that shock, fear, and curiosity might also be felt, but it is necessary to eliminate any ambiguity regarding the authenticity of the event seen on the television screen. Was it an eyewitnessed filmed or videotaped account of a collision, or was the accident part of a realistic adventure series?

The reactions to the personally witnessed street accident and the news event or fictional dramatic situation would be quite different. If the actual event were processed as if it were fiction, the consequences would be appalling. Most people can and do process information fairly accurately, but as the technology of communication media develop in sophistication and efficiency, as that technology is absorbed into the fabric of daily existence, one becomes less aware of the mediating process. The potential alteration, or perhaps obliteration, of time and space conventions affect our perception of reality.

The increasing use of videotape recording provides an intriguing example of technology's effect upon psychological processes. A common media experience serves to illustrate the point. The President of the United States addresses the American people through a live television broadcast. Time has not been altered, while space is bridged by the medium of television. Distance is dissolved through electronic connection. The viewers can be located several hundred or thousand miles away from the White House, but the event is concurrent with the distant audience's perception. The president is speaking at the very moment that individuals are watching and listening to him. The speech exists in time. Ideas through words, tone, and gesture have been developed, are developing, and will develop. Theoretically, no linguistic or environmental possibilities are locked out from potentially occurring. Happenstance is always probable. The viewer does not know what will happen as the president speaks to the nation. Indeed, the president himself, while having written the speech and planned a strategy for delivery, can never be totally sure of what will happen during the next few minutes. He might make a mistake, a technician might wander in front of the camera and distract him, nervousness could affect his concentration, an idea might suddenly occur to him as he speaks which he inserts into his prepared text. The possibilities are infinite. The tension of unpredictability always hovers over the moment.

This dramatic aspect of viewer-speaker confrontation is quite evident when contrasted with a newsclip portion of the speech included in the late evening television news coverage. The viewer knows (is conditioned by convention) that the news includes the coverage of past events, that dramatic excerpts of the speech will be shown.

Because of the existence of videotape recording, the President, for a number of reasons, might decide to prerecord his speech. He can achieve a greater degree of control by using tape. The danger of error in an important address can be totally avoided, since the address will be simply rerecorded or edited. A nervous mannerism or some slip in delivery can be eliminated. Whatever the reason, the videotaped speech is substituted for the live broadcast. Is there a difference between watching an unedited recording of the address and a live broadcast of the same event? Most people cannot distinguish a technical perceptible difference. Can you tell the difference? If both events are hypothetically identical, do psychological differences influence your perception of those two situations? Does an individual react to a recorded speech differently than to a live one?

Assume that the average person at home cannot detect a difference between the live and the taped speech and that the latter is being transmitted, but *is not identified as a videotaped event.* Obviously, there is no confusion if, merely for argument's sake, that individual is unaware of the existence of videotaping technology. It must be assumed that the broadcast is live. But awareness of the taping process requires a different psychological set. An immediate sense of ambiguity is introduced since an either/or problem now exists. Is the speech live or taped? Is it happening now? If it is taped, it is not happening now. If it is taped, where is the President of the United States while he appears on television? When was the speech recorded? If the speech is (was) taped, even though the content has not yet been revealed to the public, what will be said has already been spoken. The content of the video-taped telecast is predetermined. Therefore, the viewer's awareness of the technological means alters his relationship to the event. The viewer is no longer a participant in an actual event, since participation can never be predetermined. The viewer of the videotaped speech does not participate, but rather reacts to an orchestrated event.

Participation versus reaction is a contrast of activity and relative passivity. In that regard, the nature of the medium is relevant. In the case of film projected in a theatre, when news was an integral part of the movie theatre experience, there was never confusion about the "nowness" of the depicted event. People knew that they were watching something that had been filmed earlier. Film has to be developed, shipped to a location, and projected upon a screen by a mechanical device. The screen was not a window through which the world's events unfolded. People sense the filmic process when observing a projected image in a theatre. Film is not confused with the reality of liveness. When President Roosevelt spoke to the American people in the movie theatres during World War II it was not assumed that he was sitting in his White House office at the same time that the audience was responding to his plea for dedication and courage.

The genre of drama is a totally different matter, since it involves a special set of conventions based upon the act of self-deception which allows the fictional to assume the cloak of reality. The potency of fiction results from what Coleridge described as "the willing suspension of disbelief." Genre is, therefore, a determinant of how time and space will be processed by an audience.

Several observations can be made comparing television and film in regard to the time frame in which each medium is processed based on the technological nature of each medium. Herbert Zettl, a prominent scholar of television aesthetics, has made the comparison:

> In film the time continuum is broken down into a series of separate, discrete, frozen nows. Each frame represents an arrested now, *a state of being.* We have an accurate record of this now as it was. In reality, the film is a selection of *past* moments. *The film is a record of the past.*[2]

> In live television, the time continuum is represented by an integrated continuously moving image. The now cannot be pinpointed; it is in a

state of becoming. While each film frame is a record of the past, the *television frame is a reflection of the living present.*[3]

Just as a symbol and that which is represented are distinct, the nonfictional cinematic event ought not be confused with the photographed object. The screen is not the event, but reflects the event. In television the event exists through the screen, not on the screen. While film involves a separation in time and space (by mere definition of process), television potentially dismisses time and emphasizes space.

In television the live event invites participation because the lack of predestination gives the individual a sense of potency. If the future is not determined ahead of time, the individual can hope, wish, charm, or perhaps cast a spell that will affect what has not yet happened. Such is the case with sports fans during a tense moment of a game. They yell encouragement, perhaps knock on wood, or stroke a lucky charm, in an effort to *will* circumstances in favor of their team. The fan believes that this intense involvement can determine the course of the game. Of course, this fantasy is an illusion, an impossibility. An individual separated by miles from a contest cannot affect the outcome, but nevertheless, the rituals of partisan hopes are enacted. There is an implicit belief that the participant can influence the future. *We all play the game.* The same mechanism is at work during the broadcast of the President. To some degree, the individual viewer believes in that mysterious potential power over the event. That viewer seeks the aura of uncertainty in which he or she can cast that evil spell, disperse a blessing, or merely hope.

Televised sports events provide additional insight into how the interposition of videotape between the spectator and the game affects attitudes. The spectator at a game, a football game, for example, gets caught up in the surrounding atmosphere and usually identifies with one of the teams. It's hard to remain neutral, to detach oneself and appreciate movement and dexterity for their own sake. Eventually the spectator's neutrality is swept away by the drama. The athletic event has become the modern version of the morality play, inviting identification with the "good person" who one hopes will win over the "forces of evil." This particular relationship with the game does not change when the event is seen live on television. The contagious atmosphere of cheerleaders, the roar of the fans, the smell of excitement, are absent, but the tension of unpredictability remains, along with the morality play theme of the contest. With the magnification and editing of television, the spectator now has the best seat in the house.

Now take the same event and change one element. The entire game has been videotaped. If the viewer is unaware of the technology of videotape and actually believes that the game is live, there is no change in the relationship of viewer to game. The degree of tension has not been defused. But if the individual watches the game, knowing that it has been videotaped but not knowing the outcome, the inherent tension is relaxed a bit. A subtle change begins to occur because of the awareness that the game's outcome is predetermined, and the edge of excitement is blunted. Now the spectator is forced to "willingly suspend his disbelief" to recapture the keen excitement of "the game." "I'll pretend that it hasn't happened yet." Some people go to the trouble of hiding from newscasts and the sports section of the paper so that they will remain unaware of the outcome in order to savor and preserve the suspense of "not knowing." One other option is possible. The viewer watches a videotape of a contest which has occurred and of which he or she knows the outcome. At this point the relationship of the individual to the game changes radically. The excitement of conflict, of the unpredictable morality play, vanishes and gives way to an analytical mode of viewing. It is not a matter of who won or lost the game, but rather how the game was won or lost which is of primary importance. The morality play has given way to a display of skill. Clearly, it is the presence of videotape and the transmission of an act after it has taken place which affects the psychological relationship of viewer and event.

In the case of the president addressing the nation, the frame of reality, or the degree of "nowness," is clear when the viewer knows the speech has been taped. When there is no formal indication that the event has been taped, but the viewer is aware of the possibility that it might be taped a state of dissonance is introduced. Note that a non-videotaped program must also be identified, since an awareness of the technology suggests that *all* programs are potentially videotaped.

Because a state of ambiguity is interposed by the videotaping process, an atmosphere of cynicism and doubt lurks in the background. If videotapes are not identified or authenticated for time and date, the conclusion can be reached that *all* programs are completed and taped before transmission. Since the seeds of scepticism have been planted, when did the president actually make the speech? Hours, days, or weeks ago? If he isn't talking to us now, where is he? Could he be ill? Perhaps the country is being run by a group of individuals who control a file of prepared videotaped presidential addresses? How many people have seen the president in person within the past year? How many people have ever seen him at all? Perhaps. . . .

It is hardly possible to personally verify the existence of news events or situations outside our immediate environment. How does one check on whether something has actually occurred? Some events can be authenticated interpersonally: a question to a neighbor, a telephone call to a friend who lives where the incident took place, a quick note to an acquaintance asking for confirmation. In most situations, however, we are dependent upon media sources for information, which we verify by turning to other media sources. Cross-media checking (same medium, but different source) and intermedia confirmation (different medium) are commonplace acts which the public automatically performs. Channels are switched to find out whether the story is being covered by this news team. The importance of an event is immediately measured by the extent to which radio and television stations interrupt their normal schedules. Without on-site inspection or interpersonal verification, the average person is limited to the news media for authentication. During a time when cynicism is fashionable, an extraordinary amount of trust is placed in media organizations and people with whom the public has no immediate relationship. Is martial law in Poland a reality? Is there a civil war in Nicaragua? Was there a blizzard in Wisconsin? Was the shuttle flight aborted?

This slightly paranoic theme of distrust was dramatized in *Capricorn One,* a motion picture in which an American landing on Mars is actually staged by mission control in Houston. Writer/director Peter Hyams explained to Benedict Nightingale of the *New York Times* that he thought of the idea in 1972 when he was a reporter for CBS in New York.

> One evening he was presented a news item dealing with the Apollo program when the idea struck him: "I was thinking how easy it would be to manipulate an event in a television age. All right, you couldn't invent the Olympics, because there would be too many people watching. But there was one event of really enormous importance that had almost no witnesses. And the only verification we have that anyone reached the surface of the moon came from one camera."
>
> And was a fraudulent space-shot, he asked himself, really so very implausible? Didn't that long-unacknowledged part the United States

played in the early days of the Vietnam War indicate that such an undertaking could easily be sanctioned and organized? Think of it—a country bombing another country for eight months without anyone knowing about it. Think of all the planes involved, all the barracks that had to be built, all the beds that had to be made, all the meals that had to be cooked. My idea was peanuts beside that, much smaller in scope and scale and probability.[4]

Could a government, for the good of the people, stage the achievements of the space program? How many of you have had the idea pass through your mind just for a fleeting, doubtful moment that no American ever reached the moon? The more one thinks of it, the more plausible the idea becomes that nonconfirmable events could be manufactured for public digestion and diversion. There is an ironic aspect to that notion. Why should that possibility be more probable now, when it seems that the visual on-the-spot presence of film and television would be a more reliable source of confirmation than the idiosyncratic descriptions of newspaper journalists?

Capricorn One is a dramatic fantasy of a probable possibility, but an alleged prediction that an attempt would be made on President Reagan's life in 1981 was an actual restructuring of facts. Shortly after the March 30th attempt on the President's life, the major television news programs played an excerpt from a videotape produced at station KYNV. The section was from a show entitled *Dick Maurice and Company,* and his guest was Hollywood "psychic" Tamara Rand, who predicted that at the end of March President Reagan would be shot in the chest. It was claimed that the interview had taken place on January 6, 1981, but apparently this interview (only the relevant portion was shown on television news programs because of its sensational nature) had originally been produced on March 31, the day *after* the shooting, and had been inserted into a tape produced at an earlier time. Therefore, her amazingly accurate prediction was an elaborate hoax. Dick Maurice has since been fired by the Last Vegas television station and the Cable News Network for his complicity in the matter. Tamara Rand continues to proclaim her amazing predictive abilities.

There are probably many more examples of the distinction between actual and dramatized events becoming blurred. How are these edited, mediated events to be processed when there are no bases for judgment and no other means available for verification? How does one determine that what is currently being witnessed on the television screen is actually a newscast? Imagine turning on a television set in the middle of a program in which the news is being presented by Dan Rather or John Chancellor, but then discovering that the newscast is part of a drama about the lives of television journalists. This is really not so farfetched when you remember that in 1937 a great many panicked people could not distinguish reality from fiction during Orson Welles's radio broadcast of H.G. Wells's *The War of the Worlds.* The media world of 1937 was far less complex than that of today, and it is intriguing to contemplate whether today's media sophistication has made audiences immune to gullibility and duplicity.

Reality becomes relative when we are so dependent upon media for the structuring of our lives as we are today. The world as seen through a television screen can be real or can be a made-up construct representing reality. Staring long enough at the television screen ultimately results in a momentary thought that the sounds and images which are revealed through the set are real and that what is in front of the screen is merely illusion. Imagine staring at a television set in which you suddenly found yourself watching yourself watching a television set—certainly farfetched but not altogether impossible. The ambiguity of the television experience suggests some confusion between figure and ground. The figure-ground phenomenon involves our basic perceptual inclination to structure and organize an image by placing a less stable ground or surface against a more stable one. These printed words being read by you are perceived as being placed upon the more stable background of the white paper. When ambiguity in the figure-ground relationship is introduced, the surprises are often startling. Most people are familiar with the common psychology-book illustration of a white vase on a black background which can also be seen as the profiles of two women facing each other, depending upon your perception of which is figure and which is ground.

The correct time, place, and genre frame of television content must be understood, but the task is often surprisingly difficult and requires perseverance. That newscast into which you tuned which turned out to be a drama about the world of television journalists now turns out to *actually* be part of a documentary that is comparing images of practicing television journalists with fictional portrayals. Scenes of each have been included in the program. What is the context of the unfolding exposition and how are those scenes to be interpreted? Which is figure, which is ground?

In *Gödel, Escher, Bach: An Eternal Golden Braid,* Douglas R. Hofstadter explains that the "Strange Loop" phenomenon "occurs whenever, by moving upwards (or downwards) through the levels of some hierarchical system, we unexpectedly find ourselves right back where we started."[5] Have you ever walked into one of those cavernous stores in which the customers are monitored by a series of television cameras? It is peculiarly startling to catch a glimpse of the television monitor, which shows a strange person furtively sneaking around the counters and aisles who has an amazing resemblance to you . . . and then to realize that the figure is you and that someone else is watching, that you are under surveillance (and for a moment one is not sure whether to perform or run away). Hofstadter's description of Escher's *Print Gallery* is quite relevant here: "a picture of a picture which contains itself. Or is it a picture of a gallery which contains itself? Or of a town which contains itself? Or a young man who contains himself?"[6] All that is needed is a bit of modification, a change of medium, some imagination, and the *Print Gallery* is easily transformed into the *Television Gallery.*

Perhaps the *Television Gallery* exaggerates the confusion of reality and fiction that watching television induces in people, as if we functioned in a surrealistic fantasy world where the frames of reality were mixed in a media Mix-master. The case has probably been overstated, but where is the president?

But back to reality and a very real example of the problem. It is assumed that television newscasts are live broadcasts with filmed and videotaped news inserts introduced by a team of newscasters. Authenticity is a basic value inherent in the transmission of the news. A newscast requires a format flexible enough to allow late developments to be included. On-the-spot coverage is one of the things that distinguishes the electronic news services from newspapers and periodicals which can cover events in greater depth, but whose presentation to the public is delayed by the process of publication. Several years ago the formats and presentational style of television newscasts were altered to present to the public an atmosphere of a *real* working newsroom. The trend was to avoid the more formal, artificial, and presentational style. Often, in the background, one can see busy editors in their shirtsleeves keeping up with the latest developments as the news is being presented by the newscaster sitting in the foreground. The "real world" of pressure-packed, no-holds-barred, hard-boiled journalism recedes into the background as the news team presents the latest up-to-the minute account

of international, national, and local developments. It is therefore surprising to discover that the CBS television newscast is taped at 6:30
P.M. (Eastern Standard Time) and, while it is broadcast live to a limited
number of stations on the East Coast, most of the East Coast receives
the broadcast at 7:00 P.M. via videotape. The rest of the nation receives
a taped version later, depending on the time zone. If late items do
develop, the videotape is interrupted with a live insert. It is possible,
of course, to telecast live if necessitated by a major late-breaking news
event. To some extent, the "aura" of "immediacy" which pervades the
newscast is a facade manufactured for authenticity.

The advantage of videotape extends far beyond recording programs
which can later be telecast. As a production tool videotape allows for
material to be edited and manipulated after it has been recorded. The
implications of the editing process are complex and require some analysis. Let us examine a simple videotaped interview between two people.
A number of assumptions are made by the viewer about such a situation: the tape which is telecast is a faithful copy of the original event,
and the event was an interaction between two people which began at
one point in time and ended at a later point. These premises are valid
in the sense that the technology and conventions of television cue the
audience to process an interview almost as if it were a typical untelevised discussion between two people. The only obvious difference between an untelevised and a televised interview would be the presence
of "shots" which focus on the flow of the discussion. However, these
assumptions are quite tenuous since videotape editing can rearrange the
order of events that took place. The issue is not whether programs
should be recorded, but, rather, to what degree should tape be *edited,*
and is it the producer's responsibility to alert the audience to the editing? At the root of the problem is the audience's perception of the
interview as an unedited event and the degree of manipulation that
editing introduces. The edited event has an idealized basis existing in
real time and space. The reference is always a nonmediated situation.

The purist's position would be to object to *any* editing of videotape.
That is not the position being taken here. Editing can be a useful and
creative tool, so when is it objectionable? To answer that question, let
us return to the hypothetical interview. Scene one takes place in the
garden. The interviewee is wearing a yellow dress. The interviewer
says, "let's go into the house now." Scene two is juxtaposed to the
previous one and the interviewee is now wearing a brown dress. The

edit is obvious. There was no time (on the tape) for the pair to walk into the house. It is taken for granted that cameras and recorders stopped to allow for a change in location and dress. The viewer does not object, because the convention is understood and no one is deceived. Now the circumstances are altered slightly. Instead of recording the interview for immediate broadcast, it is recorded with the understanding that the material will be cut by half before airing (the shooting ratio is two to one). A sentence or two is eliminated. Several large sections are judged rather dull by the producers and are therefore dropped. Provocative comments made late in the interview are shifted to the beginning to grab the audience's interest immediately. Eventually the interview will be telecast, but it has now assumed the character of a "pseudo-event" (fabricated and rearranged for presentation), although it is presented as if the interaction being watched by the audience had actually once occurred in real time. The audience is not supposed to know about the procedures used to create the synthetic interaction. Those who understand the nuances of editing have no way of knowing if anything has been edited. For lack of a more descriptive phrase, this type of manipulation of an audience's perception of reality can be called "hidden tampering." It is objectionable for two reasons. First, it has no true relationship with what it pretends to be—a record of an interview between two people. It is a created situation delivered as an authentic event. Second, the producing agency generally provides no indication that editing has taken place, and a well-edited piece is very difficult to distinguish from an unedited one.

The techniques are simple, the practice common. The shooting ratios vary, but nearly all television interviews are rearranged digests of an interaction that occurred at another time and in another place. Peter Funt, writing in the *Saturday Review* discussed *60 Minutes'* production techniques.

> The *60 Minutes* library is littered with such examples of the power of television editing. And those who have fallen victim to the *60 Minutes* techniques, regardless of their culpability in whatever is being 'disclosed,' invariably express surprise at how a recorded TV segment is put together. First, they are unnerved by the film-to-air ratio of about 10-to-1, claiming, in some cases to have been worn down by the process and lulled into a false sense of security. Then, they are often startled when the interview ends and the camera is turned around to shoot so-called "reverse questions." With the camera aimed at him, the reporter

re-records all of his questions so that they may later be spliced with the answers. Although all the networks insist that reverse questions match the original questions as closely as possible, there is no denying that the reporter is allowed to polish his performance, while the interview subject's answers must stand as first delivered.

Reverse questions, along with other random shots of the reporter nodding his head or writing in his notebook, are also used to camouflage edits in the film or tape. Known as "cut-aways," these devices make a segment look smooth and neat while at the same time doing the viewers a serious disservice. When an interview subject begins a sentence, then in the middle of that sentence a cutaway is inserted of the reporter's reaction, followed by what seems to be the remainder of the subject's sentence, chances are it was never one complete sentence in the first place. The sentence was probably patched together from two parts of the interview, with the cutaway covering the break.

A producer who has worked on *60 Minutes*—who requested anonymity—says that on more than one occasion he watched Mike Wallace record an interview during which Wallace smiled and encouraged the subject to continue talking, only to insert cutaways in which Wallace has a stern, doubting expression, in effect changing the mood of the piece.[7]

60 Minutes is not being singled out here as a particular culprit, but it is a model of the practice. *All* news programs' "on-the-spot" coverage involves fragmenting an incident and restructuring the pieces into a television event. There are probably two major reasons for the practice. The economics of television place a high value on each commercial second, and air time is too valuable to be wasted. The extraneous, the interesting but insignificant, those moments of hesitation, are eliminated and destined for the oblivion of the proverbial cutting room floor—or its electronic equivalent. There is not the time or proclivity to present an extended interview. The second factor is related to the first since economic pressure increases the competitiveness of television news, and the nature of the business requires not only that a show attract an audience but also that it hold the audience and "supply" it to the program which follows. To keep the program exciting, moving, and dynamic, raw material that does not have the required energy is restructured so that the program will fulfill the criteria for viable programming. Every news program or documentary is shaped into a dramatic structure complete with crises, climax, and denouement. Each segment within a program is similarly plotted. The result is the creation of interesting, fast-developing stories, little mini-dramas produced for an audience which demands efficient absorbing programs. The producers fear that the audience might get bored! An audience weaned on such a dramatic structure ultimately begins to expect that sense of pace even from the mundane, uneventful items which must fill some of the air time. Vital people in a busy world have little time for extended conversations or media encounters; the capsulated media event fulfills the needs of the "person on the move"—an American ideal.

The Reader's Digest formula has merely been transferred to television. Shortly after Budget Director David Stockman published his criticism of President Reagan's economic policy in the *Atlantic,* members of the White House staff read copies of the article. Asked whether the President had read the article, Deputy Press Secretary Larry Speakes replied that President Reagan had still not read the piece and probably would not read it in its entirety. He would probably read excerpts. "We suggested that it would be a good way for him to read a long article."[8]

60 Minutes exemplifies the successfully produced digestible investigative journalism program. Television critic Howard Rosenberg describes this model.

> "Sixty Minutes" is a rocket. Love it. Not only is it a terrific "watch" Sunday after Sunday on CBS, but the very idea that a news-flavored hour on prime time could buck tradition and ride the top of the Nielsen ratings is wondrous and inspiring.
>
> "Sixty Minutes" created the model, set a middle-brow standard and became the definition of TV muckraking journalism that others still copy 13 years later. It is the gate-crasher that opened a path for "20/20" to prosper on ABC. It foreshadowed the present orgy of news shows and also magazine type programs that blur the line between news and entertainment.[9]

The success of the *60 Minutes* format and technique emerges out of the technology of television, film, and recording tape, which permits and encourages the manipulation and restructuring of events through the precision of digital recording and electronic editing. The difference between the accepted journalistic practices of the traditional print media and those of the electronic media is that, in television, the digested and processed is often hidden beneath the finesse and virtuosity of the technology. The assumption behind television's editing practice is that practically all content can be reduced to the essential and can be rearranged for effectiveness. In print, editing is, by definition, always assumed. The presence of the writer and editor are intrinsic to the medium and their thought is part of that which appears in print. In the world of video, effective editing means that the alteration of time and space is hidden, and the results represents the "fictionalization of the real." The symbolic nature of the visual image is overlooked, and the human presence behind the photographic icon is disregarded.

There is a need to be able to distinguish between real and artificial, between a creation of nature and a human artifact, between fantasy and reality, between what was, what is, and what will be. Just as we are impelled to classify and label objects in our environment to achieve structure and order, we should be motivated to authenticate mediated events in time and space. The lack of apparent concern over this specific issue suggests the degree to which we have abdicated sensory responsibility. Indeed, the most serious consequence is the viewer's absolution from processing the accuracy of sensory impressions. The reaction, "what difference does it make?" is symptomatic of a trend that goes far beyond narcotization. "When" and "where" are unimportant; only the construction is relevant.

The ethical dimensions of the editing process should be faced. Should it be required that a videotaped production be identified as such? Should producers be required to indicate when editing has altered a significant portion of an interview? The answer to both of these questions should be yes. Anything short of such action is manipulation. Duplicity is judgable, manipulation is not. Individuals have the ability to discern truth and falsehood. However, there is no way to distinguish an unedited videotape from a live broadcast, if minimal technical standards are maintained. There is no way to distinguish an edited conversation from an unedited one—if that is the intention of the production staff. If the audience cannot discern "then" from "now" or the "real" from the "specious," manipulation is a distinct danger and possibility. All persons have the right not to be deceived by those public institutions which serve them. The only tool available to avoid manipulation is the *proper* labeling of videotaped and/or edited productions.

Portions of this program were pre-recorded.

Which portions?

Three

The Telltale Tape, or The Video Replay and Sportsmanship

Rockne wanted nothing but bad losers. Good losers get into the habit of losing.
George E. Allen

THE CASE OF THE SHORT-HOPPED BALL

This is a tense moment, sports fans. It's the top of the ninth inning. We're ahead three to two, but they're threatening. Two outs and a man on third. A base hit will tie it up, an out and it's a giant step closer to the pennant. The outfielders are playing shallow. The play is at home. The count is full. There's the pitch and it's a wicked line drive into shallow center field and its dropping fast. I don't think he's going to get it. It'll have to be played on hop. He's got it!! No! Yes! What a play! Wait a second! There's going to be a rhubarb on this one. The opposing manager says the ball was trapped. The one ump called the man out, but the chief of the crew is being asked to overrule the decision. This argument is going to drag on for a while. We couldn't tell from up here. There's a lot at stake. Let's look at the replay. From the center-field camera it's pretty hard to tell. His body is covering the catch. Here's the angle from the first-base side. You know, it sure looks like he trapped it. Let's slow it down. Yep, there it is—the ball hits the ground first. The umps sure blew this one! But they're right most of the time. I guess we're pretty lucky, because the decision stands. The man is out. Well, you win some and you lose some. It all evens out in the end. This time we got the break. What a play by the centerfielder!!

THE TWISTED MASK

Another critical play: third down, two yards to go for a first down. The Jets are behind by three and driving. If they keep this drive alive, the momentum changes. What would you call here? The linebackers have got to make the right decision. Pass or run? There's the snap and it's a draw play right down the middle. What a hole! What a fake! And the blocking was there! Seven yards and some vicious tackling. There's a flag on the field—face masking! That's a bad penalty, because it will stop the drive. Instead of first and ten, it's third and seventeen. There's going to be a fight over this call. They better watch out or a few souls are going to be tossed out of here. There's the playback. Oh, yes. . . . It sure is face masking! See number 47's hand reaching in? Twist his head off that way—bad for the neck! It's amazing. You got to give the refs some credit. Most of the time they're going to catch the culprit! This time we didn't get away with it!

Professional and collegiate athletics are a staple of American television. While on a typical autumn Sunday 700,000 people might attend the thirteen professional football games played on that day, perhaps *thirty million* people might watch one of those games on television. A lot of rabid people are watching teams whose competitive spirit has been honed to a razorlike edge play games in which rules and a cadre of officials are necessary to maintain order. No organized games, professional or amateur, are played without the presence of officials who interpret the rules, impose penalties for violations of such rules, and conduct the movement of the contest to a conclusion.

In contrast, growing up and playing street games required a strict self-imposed code of conduct, without benefit of an outside arbiter. The need for people to supervise the game develops as its economic and/or social stakes grow in importance. That there is officiating in Little League baseball is an indication of the social importance of that athletic diversion—for participants and parents! Certainly, the trend is to introduce officiating at earlier age levels than in previous times. Five-year-old youngsters may find themselves in Pee-Wee Leagues which are patterned after professional baseball's structure and officiating.

Games always involve rules and they are always broken, sometimes accidentally, at times with intent. Did the player step on the boundary line? He or she might be unaware of the infraction. On the other hand, when the basketball player desperately grabs the opponent's uniform as the shot is being attempted, the violation of the rules is clearly intended, though perhaps not planned, but the result of a rash, impulsive strategic decision. The fouled player is therefore awarded one or two penalty shots to compensate for the violation. In organized sports the judgment of the officials is required, while in street and playground activity judgment and negotiation are the result of player participation. The consequences of rule violations involve not only the potential outcome of the game itself, but also the passionate fans and calculating gamblers. The stakes in collegiate athletics are often equal to those of professional sports. Since rules cannot be creatively improvised as the game progresses, as is common in the play of children, an administrative bureaucracy is developed which in turn appoints the official umpires and referees. There is a great deal of pressure on the officials. They must try to remain unobtrusive whenever possible, but they are never invisible: their action and decisions are public. The judgments are constant and instant—and ideally always accurate, true, and fair. But the attempt at wisdom and precision is flawed by human misjudgment and error—particularly in the frenetic circumstances and atmosphere which surround the contest.

VARIATIONS OF A GAME

Because umpires and referees do make mistakes, because the stakes are high, and because the rare poor decisions are so magnified by the public circumstances of the contest, should any available means that would help officials eliminate honest errors of judgment be used? Is there a "super referee in the sky" who can help that mere mortal? Specifically, should technology, particularly that of television, be instrumental in determining the equitable outcome of conflicts that arise because of human error?

The athletic event witnessed by people in a stadium or arena and the game seen by fans on their television screens at home are quite different. The stadium is filled with the contagious excitement generated by the contestants, by the ritual, by the thousands of other fans rooting, jeering, and yelling in support of their team and against the opposition. What is seen is determined by where you sit, the stadium design, the number of people who stand up in front of you during the big crucial play. It can be an exciting and fulfilling social experience. The fan at home has a different impression. He or she sits in the comfort of the living room without that infectious crowd or variable weather conditions (disregarding the all new weather-free plastic enclosed stadia currently being built). At home the stadium seat is not assigned, and the spectator is in the middle of the huddle one moment and then instantly behind the goal posts the next. The fan receives multiple perspectives as the television director selects a particular scene and angle from the images provided by numerous television cameras strategically placed around the playing area. Each angle is a bit different. Each image is usually magnified to some degree. A close-up of the batter's hands gripped around the bat is followed by a wide shot of the baseball diamond taken high from behind home plate. As the batter connects with the ball, the shot changes and the left fielder is seen waiting to catch the high fly. The director has the entire technology of the television medium to cover every inch of the sporting domain. Multiple cameras, variable lenses, split screens, superimposures, character-generated captions, multiple sound sources—all are part of a repertoire of techniques which get the television viewer intimately involved with the game. It is certain that the home viewer sees a more detailed view of the game, probably a more objective view than the stadium fans, the umpires, or the referees do. Added to this electronic array of video devices is videotape and the video disc which can be used to repeat plays photographed by the individual cameras.

The slow-motion disc was originally developed for use in sports coverage to permit the director to replay the action instantly at a variable speed or to stop the action in a freeze-frame.

The disc system uses a large, metallic disc pack, which rotates rapidly as the recording head system sweeps across the disc like a needle on a record turntable. . . .

The disc can record about thirty to thirty-five seconds of material at normal speed. Once the storage capacity has been reached, the unit progressively erases the older material and replaces it with new information. This allows sports productions to record the action continuously, recuing for the playback once the event is over.[1]

Slow motion, still frame, reverse motion are added to television coverage to provide a more complete, accurate, and analytical coverage of the contest. The viewer at home has more information available than the individual official (a group of officials achieve a collective view through their own specific vantage points). The home fan has far more information supplied than the poor spectator at the game who has to decipher the scoreboard hieroglyphics, the hand signals of the officials, and the muffled *basso profundo* of the public address announcer. The instant replay is the ultimate device for the transmission of athletic nuance. It transforms any home viewer into an expert, perhaps even into an unofficial umpire or referee.

The instant replay presents a dilemma for sports administrators. Why not use the television replay to facilitate equitable judgments? Admittedly, the wisdom and accuracy of most officials is highly regarded and praised by both fans and players. The officials seldom make errors, but *they are capable of error.* The knowledge of that human frailty often incites arguments which interrupt the game and generally are not resolved. A reversal of the first instant decision hardly ever occurs. The decision of the game officials is sacrosanct, although that does not eliminate intimidating demonstrative arguments. Generally, television replays corroborate the officials' decisions, but, now and then, obvious errors of judgment are revealed. "The umpire blew the call!!" Every now and than the replay indicates that the umpire or referee was mistaken. So why not help the officials by supplementing human perception with television technology?

On October 11, 1980 the Houston Astros played the Philadelphia Phillies in a National League baseball playoff game. Since that time many of the participants have gone on to other clubs and venues, but the issues remain dramatically etched in the minds of baseball aficionados. If Houston won the game they would play in the World Series, but if they lost, the playoff would be tied and the next and final playoff game would determine the representative in the World Series. This was an important game, which the Phillies won in extra innings after a contest filled with controversial plays. Such a play occurred when Garry Maddox, batting for the Phillies, hit "a soft, low liner back to the mound." the *New York Times*'s account follows:

Ruhle [Houston's pitcher] grabbed the ball at his shoe-tops and threw to first. The Phillies and many spectators apparently thought he was throwing out Maddox after having trapped the ball. But the Astros thought they were doubling Trillo off first. In the confusion, McBride ran to third and stood there for a few moments. Finally, Art Howe, the Houston first baseman, who still had the ball, ran to second and ostensibly tripled McBride off the bag.

Did Ruhle catch the ball and was it a triple play? [italics author's] The argument raged for 20 minutes on several fronts. Doug Harvey, the homeplate umpire and considered one of the strongest in the business, went to the front-row box seats near the Astro dugout and consulted Charles (Chub) Feeney, the president of the National League. Even Schmidt, the third baseman [for the Phillies] went over and consulted Feeney.

The crowd was still howling when the decision was announced: the pitcher caught the ball and doubled Trillo off first, but McBride was unfairly tripled off second.

"I was screened out," he said, "and didn't see the play. The umpires at first base and third were discussing the play, so time was technically out and the third out is not allowed."

Half a loaf satisfied neither manager. Green protested the game for the Phillies, and Bill Virdon protested it for the Astros. When play resumed, Larry Bowa hit the first pitch to second for the third out.

Later Feeney issued this statement: "Doug Harvey said he was blocked out by the runner and called it no catch. The first-and-third-base umpires ruled it no catch. The first-and-third-base umpires ruled it a catch. Harvey said that because he made the no-catch sign, he probably confused the runner at second. So he put him back on second. They're a very good crew of umpires, they know the rules. I have to concur that their decision was correct.[2]

According to ABC television director Dennis Lewin, no one looked at the tape to resolve the controversy. Replays do not *always* provide the clear answer: the angle might be off, another player could get in the way and block the camera's vision, the shot might not be magnified enough. Nevertheless, it is somewhat surprising to see that they carefully avoided using the tape as a source of additional information. It is equally significant, and *obvious,* that the one person in the ballpark who would have the definitive answer, the pitcher, was never asked whether he caught or trapped the ball. That conspicuous omission reveals a great deal about the value system operating in athletics.

FOR ARGUMENT'S SAKE

Professional athletes' reactions toward the possible use of video replays to help officials in difficult situations are generally negative. Joe Torre, former manager of the Atlanta Braves, insists that the replay would *hurt* baseball, that it would take the argument, an integral part of the game, out of it. Chuck Tanner, former manager of the Pittsburgh Pirates, responded similarly:

> No! I don't think replays ought to be used. It depends upon what angle is shown. It can be very deceptive. You look at a guy sliding into second and on one replay he will be safe. You catch him the other way and he looks like he's out. It would take a lot away from the game. I think the umpire's a human being just like the player. They're going to make mistakes, but they are going to try. It would take the personal part away from the fans and from all aspects of the game. I don't think the game should be changed in any way. To me the replay would be the worst thing you could do because, why not have them on balls and strikes? That wouldn't tell you a thing either. Let's keep the game with the people.

In response to whether arguments were a necessary part of the game, Tanner said, "we only argue on the ones where we think we're right. *If we think we got the guy* [italics mine]."

Harvey Haddix, pitching coach for Pittsburgh, agreed that the various replay angles could be misleading and that their use would take something away from the game.

> I think the element of doubt is always something that's good. Arguing has always been part of the game and always will be. There are always going to be disagreements if things don't go your way. To me this is part of the game. As long as it's a legitimate argument, the fans love it.

Does the ballplayer argue even if he knows he's wrong?

> If he can convince somebody otherwise, more power to him. If he can convince the umpire that he did catch the ball or some other umpire, and you'll get disagreement in umpires once in a while, because each one of them sees something from a different angle and it's never really sure whether the guy caught the ball or not, or whether he short-hopped it or not. And the same thing at second base on a steal. Did he get under the tag? Was he ahead of it? Nobody will ever know. That doubtful question is part of the game. It makes it more interesting.

The players agree that arguments are part of baseball tactics and are a vital part of the game. They also agree that while tape is an invaluable asset because it can be used to spot problems of execution and technique, it creates an atmosphere of intimidation if used in officiating. Joe Pignatano, former Met coach, stated that, in his opinion, replays would harm the efforts of the umpire.

> I don't think they should use replays, because it openly criticizes the man who makes the decision, whether it's wrong or right. If you show instant replays and show that the umpire has made a mistake, that man is going to catch hell the whole rest of the day.

Of course, what is being objected to is the use of the instant replay as an aid in officiating. There is no objection voiced to letting the viewer *at home* see possible errors of judgment.

In basketball the quickness of pace adds to the officials' problems. Two officials watching the moves of ten players on the court (and sometimes the bench) cannot catch every violation that occurs as the players race up and down the court. In response to the question whether videotape replays might be helpful, Butch Beard, a former NBA player for several teams, including the New York Knicks, replied,

> Most of the guys, the officials, call the game on instinct and good judgment. More than 80 percent of the time they are right.

But Beard's response was not unequivocal and left room for the use of the replay in crucial playoff series. Sly Williams, former Knickerbocker forward, felt that the replay would eliminate some important elements of the game.

> It would take the fun out of the game and take away the official's right to make a call. He's human and should be allowed to make a mistake, because we make mistakes out there. People make mistakes every day. It would not be good to use the videotape replay to judge a man for the calls he makes in a split instant. Sometimes they're wrong, but they do a hell of a job out there and most of the time they're right.

Williams also indicated that the officials' fallibility serves the strategy of the game. "They can't call every little foul. So you do get a chance to get a guy here and there and throw him off. If you do get caught, you know you can't go that far next time."

Former coach Red Holtzman's response also stressed the need to preserve the possibility of error: "The reasons for accuracy are great, but I think that you are taking away some of the human element that the referees supply as well as the players." He maintains that electronically aided officiating would not work in the game of basketball.

> I don't think the people, maybe they do, but speaking for myself, I don't want to come and see everything pat, cut, and dried. I want to go there and be surprised. I hate to see a bad call in basketball or football, or anything else. You hate to see an important game won because some guy made a mistake, but that's still part of it.

In football similar concerns have been expressed about using the replay. Sports columnist Joe Falls was passionate in his voiced disapproval.

> Should they use instant replays in judging those plays?
> And I give you the old answer: No. Absolutely no. A thousand times no.
> For whatever good will come out of it, such a procedure will create far more harm.
> We will be replacing people with machines and that's never worked yet, in any society, for any reason.
> In the end, people prevail." [3]

There are a few people who suggest that some attempt be made to help the officials in their difficult, almost impossible task. Sports columnist Larry Felser asks "wouldn't it benefit the officials to have an electronic aid so they could be helped out of thorny predicaments?" [4]

> That's not a rap at the competence or the integrity of NFL [National Football League] officials. It's just that the pressure of these games is too much for the naked eye in many cases. In an era when game plans are produced by computers and science is virtually on the roster, why should the officials be asked to operate as if it were 1948? [5]

The arguments for any use of television replays to help officials are overwhelmed by a deluge of voices seeking to protect the sanctity of the particular sport. The strongest and most vocal opponents are the administrators of the major professional leagues. Pete Rozelle, Commissioner of the National Football League, states:

> The games would be lengthened and boredom would result if instant replays were called upon to settle every coach's beef. Different camera angles often give the same play different interpretations, and the cost of camera equipment would discourage many club owners from installing it. [6]

Nevertheless, in the summer of 1979 the National Football League initiated a trial run of a replay system during the exhibition season, but all twenty-eight professional clubs concluded that it was not feasible. It was, however, *not* ruled out for the future. During the trial run 166 plays were studied over seven games. Consulting those plays, 23.7 per game, by the officials added eleven minutes to each game. Of the 166 replays, 54 percent supported the officials' calls, 42 percent were inconclusive, and 4 percent might have resulted in the reversal of the call.[7] Since that time a number of experiments have been introduced, but the game remains essentially free of electronic officiating.

In March 1986 the NFL voted for a 1-year system of limited instant replays in which only "indisputable visual evidence" would be used to reverse an on-field decision. The "limited" system excludes most infractions and concentrates on plays of *possession* or *touching*.

There are sporting events in which electronics do play an important role. Horse racing and many track events have used motion picture film and photographs to determine finish line decisions or to spot violations that might have occurred during the race. In swimming events electronic touch plates are used to determine exact timings. It is curious that electronics are effective in some sports and not in others. Bud Greenspan offers an explanation:

> Film is suitable to horse racing because these controversies are decided *after* the event is completed. In sports such as football, basketball, boxing, baseball, tennis and ice hockey, controversies are always occurring and must be ruled upon while the game is in progress. This alone makes the delay of the play impractical and, even more, unfair.[8]

More recently, electronic technology has been introduced into tennis and was first used at Wimbledon and in the United States Open Championship in 1980. A combination of electric eye and judges determined whether the serve was in or beyond the service line.

Although television viewers all over the world are privy to the insights provided by television technology, the officials and participants vow to keep video replays out of sports. The argument is capsulized by Bud Greenspan.

> Athletes are human. So are officials. If we cannot expect perfection from the performers, how can we expect more from those who officiate? The structure of sports is based on the premise that all one can ask of an athlete is that he or she be dedicated, prepared, talented, and courageous. Can anyone doubt that these qualifications do not hold true for officials?[9]

The expressed attitudes are understandable. One cannot help being sympathetic with a position which elevates human interaction over technological dependency: an expression and recognition that human beings are capable of mistakes—particularly in the heat of athletic contests. The mistake and the reverberating effects—anger, argument, and conflict—are professed to be "part of the game." On the other hand, technological mistakes, when machines fail, are abhorred. The tautology follows that machines are never allowed to make mistakes because they are not human. The sports arena is portrayed as a haven from the technology that has affected almost every other sector of public life (including the administration, coaching, planning, and financing of the sports institution itself) but has been barred from entering the game itself, which must remain pure—the confrontation of person against person or of an individual against odds and time.

But the image of organized sports as free of the taint of media technology is illusory, since the television viewers (the overwhelming majority of spectators) see a game that is altered by electronic techniques used to transmit an interesting, commercial viable form of entertainment into the home. While the participants and administrators of the game maintain a "hands-off" policy in regard to the use of television as an official's secondary tool, the home viewer's relationship with the game is altered because of the intimate and revealing nature of the medium. The television viewer has been transformed into a participating expert who sees every visible nuance of the game. The "Monday morning quarterback" has been replaced by "Tele-coach," who plays and controls the game as if he or she were actually coaching or managing the athletes. Every move is appreciated. Nothing escapes the camera's eye. "The timing is off on the hand-off." "The curve didn't break." "He moved before the snap of the ball." "That was icing!" A new relationship, a new appreciation, a different game has been created for the viewer at home. The nature of the game and our attitudes toward the rules that govern it need to be examined because television superimposes another ethical structure over our concept and tradition of "sportsmanship."

SPORTSMANSHIP

The television spectator, who has more information available about what is going on than anyone else at the game, has shifted his/her allegiance as a new coalition has formed, uniting player and fan against the common enemy, the person who puts it all on the line with great risk, the vulnerable game official. The development of this "new" coalition requires a redefinition of "sportsmanship."

An athletic event has an ethical structure which is manifested in a set of rules that are established to govern the game. The model of player interaction has traditionally stressed honesty and the development of character. That model is very much intertwined with the democratic ideal of "fair play and good sportsmanship." John Richard Betts, writing about *America's Sporting Heritage* states:

> Americans of every walk of life increasingly recognized the potential value of sports as a promoter of the democratic spirit. . . . Fair play demands that all who participate in the contest must abide by the rules, and in sports the competitor is most sharply confronted with this necessity.[10]

The paragon of the virtuous life, the exemplar of sports as a character builder, is Frank Merriwell of "Fardale Academy, Yale College and the world at large. He was the unreal ideal."[11] Gilbert Patton, who created the character, saw Frank Merriwell standing for "truth, faith, justice, the triumph of right, mother, home, friendship, loyalty, patriotism, the love of *alma mater,* duty, sacrifice, retribution and strength of soul as well as body."[12]

The ideal that proclaimed honor and sportsmanship was tested on the playing field. How one conducted oneself on the playing field was an indication of potential beatification. One of the most famous descriptions of the sporting code was written by the dean of American sports writers, Grantland Rice:

> For when the One Great Scorer comes
>   To write against your name
> He writes—not that you won or lost—
>   But how you played the game.[13]

The etiology of "sportsmanship" is difficult to trace. *Webster's Sports Dictionary* defines the term as

> the ethical behavior exhibited by a sportsman or athlete. Good sportsmanship is generally considered to involve participation for the pleasure gained from a fair and hard-fought contest, refusal to take unfair advantage of a situation or of an opponent, courtesy toward one's opponent, and graciousness in both winning and losing.[14]

The Oxford English Dictionary defines "sportsmanship" as "the performance or practice of a sportsman; skill in, or knowledge of, sport;

conduct characteristic of a sportsman."[15] The term was used by George Farquhar in 1706 in *Beaux Stratagem,* in which the following exchange occurs: *Atm.* "A sportsman, I suppose? *Bon.* Yes sir, he's a man of pleasure; he plays at whist and smokes his pipe eight-and-fifty hours together some times."[16] Somewhere along the way the meaning of "sportsmanship" changed from participation in a particular practice to cultural ideal. The *Oxford Universal Dictionary* indicates the spectrum and evolution of usage:

> 1. A man who follows, engages in, or practices sport; esp. one who hunts or shoots wild animals or game for pleasure. 2. U.S. A gambler, betting man 1848. 3. *trans.* One who displays the typical good qualities of a sportsman 1984. Hence Sportsmanlike a, resembling a s.; like that of a s.; consonant with the character of a s.[17]

The point at which "honor and ethical behavior in playing the game" becomes a commonly held societal value is most difficult to trace. For some the rules of the game were symbolic of social interaction. For others the sporting scene represented a rigid structure whose rules could not be violated without sanction, and punishment, because without rules the game could not exist. The game and its rules were training for "real life." Therefore, children were taught that it was wrong to cheat, that the rules had to be obeyed, and that sportsmanship was part of the democratic ideal.

Why does the concept of sportsmanship have such a hollow ring today? Do we no longer heed the rules of the game? Or has the contest become a test of the ability of the participants to see how far they can go without being caught violating the rules? Does sportsmanship have a different meaning for spectator and participant? In *Man, Sports, and Existence: A Critical Analysis,* Howard S. Slusher states that "sports is integrally concerned with the business of achieving. And in so doing, the act must be one of volition in order to be truly moral."[18] Accordingly, sportsmanship does not *belong* to the game, because to be sporting does "not reflect the essence of the game."[19]

> To even hint that the "Christian ethic" is to be maintained in modern sport is to contradict the very existence of sport as we know it. At the risk of sounding greatly "used," I must indicate that in sports, traditional *Christian ethics are dead.* One simply cannot expect two tennis players to place their shots in such a position, provided they did possess the necessary skill, as to assist in the increased development of the opponent. This is imply not the reason for sports as we know it today. The name of the game is win.[20]

Slusher maintains that sports is not the place to teach morals and ethics, but it is an encounter in which the human being realizes the self through action and impulse. Thus to maintain "sportsmanship" as a value is naive and unrealistic.

> Grantland Rice was noble, but wrong, when he indicated that they remember you for "how you played the game." They remember you for sixty-one home runs, 9.1 seconds in the 100-yard dash, 10-foot vaults, four-minute miles, and over one-hundred stolen bases. Mr. Durocher, in saying that "nice guys finish last" might have been right, but that is only because he confused values with placement.[21]

Whether sportsmanship is an archaic value of the past, a shibboleth, or whether it is an integral part of a belief system depends, in part, on attitudes toward winning and the view toward those rules which govern the game. Unsportsmanlike behavior requires the violation of those rules which define the contest. Rules, according to Rosenfield, Hayes, and Frentz in *The Communicative Experience,* serve two functions: "they *constitute* the game," because its structure emerges out of the formulation of a code which defines the game, and "they regulate behavior appropriate to the game."[22] Rules regulate by providing limitations on behavior and by providing sanctioned punishment for violations. A set of arbitrary rules governs the action of the game's participants during a set period of time. The rules "are merely the formal preconditions of a game (the game's focus of attention is the activity occurring within the limited)."[23] When, however, the need for rules becomes paramount, their violation is also accentuated.

The Art of Violation

The present exercise in comedy which once was called wrestling is characterized by the spectators' major preoccupation with the violation of the former sport's rules. The wrestlers have been transformed into actors who assume the roles of heroes and villains. The audience, once known as spectators, pretend that the exhibition is really a match, and the crises of this minidrama revolve around the efforts of the antagonist to pulverize, maim, and annihilate the protagonist, using every illegal means available, without being caught by the harrassed referee. The illegal means are never hidden from the audience, but only from the ring official. The heinous villain displays his illegal and evil techniques with great skill and aplomb. The former athletic event receded into the background because the gross violations of the rules redefined the contest. Note that the presence of rules is still an absolute necessity, because without regulations illegality would have no substance. In professional wrestling, physical ability and courage in combat have given way to style and degree of violation. How skillful was the person in violating the rules of the game? The metamorphosis of wrestling is in all probability linked with the popularity of that sport in the early days of television. The entrepreneurs quickly realized that traditional wrestling would bore an audience and that flamboyant action would be far more appealing. The wrestlers themselves learned quickly how to play to the magnifying lenses of the intimate television camera. But professional wrestling cannot be taken seriously any longer as an athletic event, although its transformation is indicative of how attitudes toward the rules and the sporting event can change.

Every game participant is forced into a position of choice: whether to violate the rules or not. Every athlete faces a dilemma.

> Each player must adjust his or her game behavior to accommodate two contrary impulses: (1) striving to win the game while (2) striving to maintain the integrity of the game.[24]

Winning is important, but whether the game is played honestly *ought* to be equally relevant. Quite clearly some people "cheat" in order to win. "But to cheat is to defy the rules of the game and therefore to threaten the viability of the game itself."[25] The problem becomes even more complex, because cheating's protean forms make it very difficult to define. In "Cheating in Sports" Guenther Lueschen states that "cheating in sports is the act through which the manifestly or latently agreed upon conditions for winning such a contest are changed in favor of one side."[26] There are many variations of cheating, some of which are not relevant here. We are concerned with the public event, the play on the field, not with the publicly undetectable violations of the game such as bribed players shaving points for gamblers, or athletes ingesting illegal drugs such as steroids to increase their performance capability. Faking classroom credits to be eligible for collegiate teams is a serious violation, but we are preoccupied *only* with violations that occur within the context of the game, and which would, under the best of all possible circumstances, be found or spotted by the game officials at the time of their occurrence. There are two major categories of game infractions:

the first occur because of game circumstances and are either accidental or intentional; the second involve unethical conduct and cheating. Moving before the snap of the football can be accidental; touching the soccer ball with one's hand can often not be avoided; moving with the basketball and not dribbling is common and can result from poor coordination or sheer momentum. Some violations are deliberate, although not premeditated. In football, holding on to the face mask of the opposing player is illegal. Some players resort to it only as a desperate move to avoid a long gain or a touchdown, although others use the tactic constantly while hoping that it goes unnoticed by the officials. The latter act borders on unethical conduct. Premeditation is difficult to determine and requires the on-the-spot judgment of the officials. In some sports, additional sanctions are meted out if the violation is believed to have been flagrant and deliberate.

Violating the rules does not always mean cheating or unsportsmanlike conduct. At times breaking rules is considered a viable strategy and part of the art of playing the game well. The foul shot in basketball is awarded precisely because a rule is violated, either intentionally or unintentionally. As the forward drives along the base-line he is jostled by the guarding player and misses the attempted shot. The offender is charged with a foul and the interfered player is awarded two penalty shots. If five fouls (six in the professional league) are collected, the player has to leave the game. It is "smart" defense to make sure that the opponent's "easy" shot is obstructed by committing a deliberate foul because the odds that the player will miss the penalty shots might outweigh the apparent easy layup shot. It is "smart" offense to draw a foul from the defensive player.

An impending goal in hockey is often avoided by tripping the offensive player with a hockey stick. It is part of the game's strategy; it is "smart" hockey, to draw the penalty rather than accept the inevitable goal. Breaking rules can be a legitimate and creative part of many games. That is, a player's and coach's ability to manipulate rules is a matter of skill which can alter the outcome of the contest.

If breaking the rules is condoned and appreciated by the participants, officials, and spectators, what constitutes ethical or unethical game playing? If violating rules is proper strategy, what is unsportsmanlike conduct? Most sports distinguish between breaking the game's rules and unsportsmanlike conduct, creating a different set of sanctions. With some exceptions, flagrant violence is not condoned, although it is appreciated by a large proportion of the fans, players, and coaching staff. Despite the increasing anxiety being expressed about violence in sports, particularly in professional hockey, brutality continues to fascinate fans. Nevertheless, some physical acts are not part of the game and exist outside the formal rules that constitute the event. Indeed, it is as if an unwritten code of "rules of revenge" coexisted with the accepted operational prescriptions. The "beanball" pitch in baseball (deliberately throwing at the batter), kicking a soccer player, piling on a fallen football player, or hitting the opponent over the head with a hockey stick, are considered gross and outrageous, but sometimes necessary, acts. Such incidents occur regularly—not without provoking glee in the stands and sneers of retribution from the bench.

The change television has brought about in the spectator's relationship to the game and the rules which govern it has also influenced attitudes toward concepts of fair play and sportsmanship. Even in amateur Little League games the influence of television exposure can be seen as the participants imitate the mannerisms and techniques of their adult counterparts. The strut, the batting swing, the uniform paraphernalia—batting and sliding gloves, wrist bands, etc.—and the attitudes toward "fair play" mirror stadium ritual. "Breaking the rules" has become central to playing the game. The television camera and the videotape replay emphasize and isolate violations which go undetected by the game officials but are obvious to the television spectator. The isolating camera has elevated violation to a parity position with individual athletic performances. The virtuosity of the multiple-angled instant replay equals violation with skill.

A baseball game is televised with six cameras: three umpires officiate. The viewers' response to an undetected violation is fairly predictable. The fan at home automatically begins to second-guess the officials by calling balls and strikes, close plays, fouls, violations, out of bounds plays. At the same time, the television spectator is also a fan taking sides and rooting for a team or a player. If the home team, or the group for which the fan is rooting, has suffered the consequences of a detected violation, some sense of relief and jubilation is felt when justice is administered. If, however, the member of the "other" side manages to get away with a flagrant infraction, anger is expressed at both the culprit who was responsible for the awful deed and the officials who did not respond by handing out punishment. A variation of that response is to marvel at the skill of the players who manage to fool the officials and deplore the incompetent official who allowed the perpetrator to get away with an obvious foul. The basketball player aware that the referee's view is shielded by another player pokes an elbow in the ribs of the guarding opponent. The first baseman, knowing that the umpire is looking at the base and listening for the sound of the baseball hitting the mitt, slaps his mitt with his hand to confuse the official. The infringements are openly displayed to all but the ruling officials. The conflict one would expect a fan who witnesses a violation on television to feel is disarmed by the shift in attitude toward the incident. Instead of being regarded as an ethical issue, the violation is now considered an accomplishment. Does the player get away with it? How accomplished is he or she in the act?

Central to the entire sporting event are the isolated game officials whose responsibilities have become increasingly complex and difficult to execute. "The referee acts as the visible controlling agent . . . of law enforcement in sport. He watches the proper conduct of a game and continuously deals out sanctions in order to secure equality of chance and a just outcome."[27] The referee's or umpire's mandate is limited to the observable playing field, but his or her actions and decisions are scrutinized, analyzed, and criticized by players, spectators, sports commentators, television viewers, and anyone else who wishes to join in the fun. Game officials are pitted against both players and audience who judge their capability in discovering infractions and dispensing justice within a peculiar code of conduct determining player–official relationships. That code includes some fairly clear stipulations. (1) Never help the umpire arrive at a decision. The burden of proof always rests with the official. (2) Close calls warrant a public argument. While decisions are rarely ever reversed, most managers and players agree that the argument serves to intimidate the official in future situations. Notice that the argument is never private, since it is choreographed for the person seated in the deepest recesses of the stadium and for the home viewer who is right there in the middle of the harangue. The histrionics of a Billy Martin or an Earl Weaver go far beyond an interpersonal disagreement, but are rhetorical strategies to be understood by all who witness the situation. (3) Break the rules whenever it serves the strategic purposes of the game and hide the violation from the game officials, but do it well. (Unskilled violations are not appreciated by the fans, particularly the fans at home.) (4) The teammate is always to be supported and is never wrong in any disputation with an opponent or an official.

Most players and managers acknowledge that the officials do an extraordinary job, under circumstances that require a fixed and inflexible ethical stance while the other participants' attitudes are determined by game conditions and extenuating circumstances. The official must be consistent while the players erratic behavior is the result of *the contest.* Adding to the difficulty of the official's task is the videotape replay which provides the home viewer with hindsight and wisdom. The multiangled replay is shown during the field arguments. While the disagreement is played out by participants, coaches, and officials, the television viewer role-plays his or her own private argument, based upon the replay, and is perversely satisfied if all indications are that the "ref" or "ump" blew the call.

THE ELECTRONIC STADIUM

"Never before have so many witnessed so few make such obvious mistakes." The expectations of the television fan have invaded the baseball stadium experience. Television's instant replay, slow motion, split screen, statistics, instantaneous measurements of pitching speed, biographies, highlights, interviews, players' comments, close-ups, and play-by-play commentary soon began to be missed in the stadium. Team owners and arena administrators soon recognized fans' expectations. Clearly, the sight of stadium fans balancing their small television sets on their laps indicated the need for future innovation. The result has been, of course, to electrify the stadium and arena by redesigning the scoreboard and adding giant video displays. "If you can't beat television, bring it into the game." "Diamond Vision," at Shea Stadium in New York, is an example of the newer sophisticated stadia electronic devices which have been introduced into some sports arenas. It allows for the presentation of pictures of the ballplayers, up-to-date statistics, live "coverage" of the fans, messages, animated graphics, and plays. The operator can choose from special designated stadium cameras or any one of the signals used for broadcasts. Any of these signals can be instantly shown on the stadium's giant screen, and any portion of a videotape chosen by the programmer can be replayed or still-framed. In 1977, in reaction to the use of a monochromatic predecessor of Diamond Vision in the Atlanta stadium, the umpires walked out momentarily in protest because a close play had been replayed on the screen. Such a situation was considered much too volatile. They were somewhat appeased when a former umpire was placed in the booth with the power to decide if a play was too controversial to be shown to the stadium spectators.

However, the controversy continued. When the replay was introduced in Shea Stadium in 1982 the umpires balked and let it be known that they were unhappy with any situation in which their judgment would potentially be questioned. Jim Kearney, Director of Diamond Vision for the New York Mets, issued a statement that the National League office was examining the situation, but in the meantime no replays would be shown if (1) they might lead to arguments, (2) they might incite fans and possibly cause a riot, or (3) if a ruling has already been disputed. These guidelines have remained. Sports columnist Dick Young reacted in his *New York Post* story, "Umps Way Out Of Line On Replays."

> LORDS OF BASEBALL GUILTY of another gutless action. In order to avert strikes of umpires on Opening Day, both leagues agreed that there would be no replays of close calls on ballpark video boards. Thus, we had [the] ludicrous situation the other day where umpire Nick Colosi interrupted a Mets ballgame to order that the control room stop showing a slomo [slow motion] to the customers. It just so happens that on this particular play, as on most, the ump who made the call had it right. But the critical issue is this: a ballclub spends $4 million to construct a huge video screen to serve the fans, and then is told by the umpires that such service cannot be given. I reject [the] umps' contention that such replays might infuriate fans and lead to violence. They have become rabbit-eyed as well as rabbit-eared. Putty-kneed owners, by giving in, now have reached [the] point where players and umpires run their ballparks.[28]

While millions of individuals at home have the privilege and advantage of second-guessing the umpires, the spectators at the game itself are limited to the impressions of their nontechnologically aided senses. In an anachronistic dilemma, the umpires defend their ability to administer justice and preserve the integrity of the game, while their ability to discern dishonesty and cheating is judged by those at home and in the stadium who see the game through the hindsight of television technology.

The consensus of athletes, administrators, and sport officials is that the videotape replay *as an officiating tool does not belong in the game.* Some feel that further experimentation is warranted and that perhaps the replay could be incorporated on a limited or restricted basis as an aid. But there is an overwhelming litany of objections to the proposal: the expense, its elimination of the fun of argument, the delays, the fallibility of videotape, and the insult to the umpire's or referee's professionalism and accuracy. The arguments are understandable, and one cannot help but be sympathetic with the effort to preserve the purity, the essence, the vitality of a specific sport. Yet for some, the sincere attempt to preserve the "true" tradition is perceived as arrogance in the face of developing technology and contrary evidence.

THE END OF SPORTSMANSHIP?

The athletic event is a vestige of the past, of a preindustrial world, one in which courage, vitality, strength, suppleness, and dexterity existed without the benefit of "extra-human" devices or the technical ingenuity the human race was developing. That romantic notion encompasses not only the competing athletes, but also the officials who adjudicate the proceedings. It is the symbolism of this pure act of physical prowess and courage which clashes with the dissemination by the media and its facilitating technology of those heroic acts. At some point sports involvement became divided into participants and spectators. A spectator's appreciation requires an aesthetic distance and that television has dissolved. The new sports coalition is the result of the penetration of participation by the nonparticipants.

Lurking in the background is the question, what constitutes ethical behavior or sportsmanship in athletics? The innocuous acts on the sporting field are symbolic models of values and behavior. It has always been that way, except now the impact is magnified by television. Do athletic events as they are presented on television represent the ideals of ethical behavior and sportsmanship? Consider some common responses: "American sports merely mirror the state of the society, and the unsportsmanlike, often brutal, behavior witnessed on television is a realistic analogue of life in the real world," or "Sports prepare young people for the harder realities of life, and organized athletics therefore serve as needed models." The answer you are *least* likely to get is that sports represent a moral training round, or that sportsmanship is a highly esteemed value which guides us in our interaction with others.

If sportsmanship has become nothing but an American shibboleth then the domination of televised sports has contributed to its demise as a value. The cynicism of exploitation is difficult to reconcile with a tradition of honesty and virtue in organized sports.

> *You learn to cheat a little bit. That's what its all about.*
> A professional athlete

Four
Walls of Sound

One very cold night a group of porcupines were huddled together for warmth. However, their spines make proximity uncomfortable, so they moved apart again and got cold. After shuffling repeatedly in and out, they eventually found a distance at which they could still be comfortably warm without getting pricked. This distance they henceforth called decency and good manners.

Edward O. Wilson, *Sociobiology: The New Synthesis*

The dental-medical suite: its peculiar ambience is immediately recognizable to the visitor. The empty waiting room is separated from the official world by a sheet of glass behind which people in white peer without remorse or emotion at the human specimen who is about to meet the inscrutable medical establishment. It is the usual doctor's office equipped with copies of *Reader's Digest* and *National Geographic* (actually there is a correlation between the status of the physician, the slickness of the available reading matter, and the amount requested on the bill). A sign asks the patients not to smoke and, because of the cost of bookkeeping, requests payment of bills on the spot. But what characterizes the space more than anything else is the sound that takes the place of the cacophony of the less ordered world which has been left outside. Instead of cars, sirens, drills, jackhammers, and the mysterious unclassified murmurs of the city, the sounds of pleasant strings waft through the air. The music cannot be identified, but goes along with the rest of the air-conditioned decor. All over the United States people are entering the acoustically purified sanctum of their physician's office, shuffling to the beat of languid sound that is oozing out of hidden speakers controlled by the great sound master in the sky—the book-keeper-nurse-amanuensis in white and keeper of the dial. Other patients enter, sit, nod, but do not speak to anyone else, as if idle talk were against the house rules or would violate the aura of illness which hangs over each person's head. It is as if the room and its sound regulated relationships, insulating each person from the others' germs and personalities. Now and then a door opens and the nurse announces a name and a room number. This is it! Audition time! The patient is led into examining room number two with instructions to strip and put on a white paper antiseptic robe. This act completed, there is nothing else to do but stare at the paraphernalia, which includes an ugly examining table, complete with stirrups, and instruments that are stuck up every possible orifice of the human body with as much pain and stretching as possible (sitting alone stimulates medical fantasies!). On the table are syringes, vials, salves, and the rest of the scientific accoutrements which are there to aggravate any medical encounter. Equally prominent in this claustrophic domain is the musical atmo-sphere of the waiting room. The beat and tempo have not changed. There is the speaker and the dial that controls the sound which enters the examining room. A Verdi requiem might be appropriate, certainly not pseudo-Montavoni-Beach Boy-strings!

The impulsive act now occurs as I turn off the music which is beginning to add to my illness. All the channels provide the same uni-form baths of sound, and one dial controls the volume which was gently turned until I was alone with my misery. A stunning moment of silence, except for humming air conditioner, an occasional ringing tele-phone, the opening and closing of doors, and what might be inter-preted as muffled gasps or sobs. Suddenly the door opens and there is the doctor, but his first act is not to greet me or even to look at the folder his efficient nurse left on the table for him providing him with my name and medical history. His first response is to turn the dial and return the room to normalcy. Music must accompany the examination!

Besides wondering whether the sound of my heart would be heard over the music, or if some confusion might result between those subtle musical beats and my more human ones, I began to consider the impact of the recorded music that accompanies us everywhere we go, some-times by choice, but often without consent. The airplane attached to the ground world by some sort of umbilical cord while parked at the terminal is filled with music, indicating that the passengers are still psychologically connected to the safe world of the terminal. Once the plane disembarks and before a choice of seven or eight earphone sound environments can be purchased, the passenger is conspicuously transferred to a new musical environment controlled not by the terminal, but by the plane itself. The strategy is clear, reassure the passenger of safety by controlling the acoustical environment.

Some hotel and restaurant bathrooms purr out soothing sounds, thereby masking the actual functions performed. A telephone call to a corporate office or to an airline that is placed on hold is automatically switched to a musical purgatory. The abrasive sound of the alarm clock has been replaced by one of many radio station formats, including "top forty," "easy listening," "Jazz," "country," "rock," and "classical." The jogger runs in the privacy of a musical world. A walk along the street or a ride in a public transport involves interactions with a succession of musical spheres. A car passes by with a blaring radio. Someone walks by carrying a portable stereophonic AM-FM cassette deck which has the capability of blasting forth at an extraordinary volume. Heads and homes have been converted to concert halls with stereophonic headphones and multiple speakers. Who would drive an automobile without an AM-FM radio and perhaps a cassette player, CB capability, and stereophonic sound? The apartment house or office building elevator is filled with passengers who seek to ignore each other and the filtered-in-music during their ninety-second ride. Our lives are inextricably connected with the media of public sound.

Music is important to most people—it has always been so—except today one *never* has to be without musical accompaniment. The availability of recorded music has transformed the exceptional into the usual and has brought into conflict the human urge for privacy with the equally strong desire for connection and accompaniment. While most members of a democratic society would uphold the principle of freedom of expression, that principle is not absolute and has its limits. The collision of freedom of expression with the right to silence is apparent when choice is eliminated and one is forced to listen to other people's music.

The push-button car radio, transistors, and magnetic tape recording are part of a culture which stresses mobility along with auditory connection. You don't have to remain stationary to listen to music. The radio has been shrunk from a piece of furniture to a compact item which can be carried, worn, and hidden during any activity. A day at the seashore without a radio or cassette player is an idiosyncratic act violating the prescribed rules of beach conduct. For some, pounding surf has been overpowered by the sounds of radio stations and audio cassettes. For others, the roar of the waves has been replaced by a plugged in soundscape heard through earphones.

The introduction of stereophonic recordings and receivers transformed the living room by replacing the one piece of furniture with a series of components that would dominate the room along with the television set. The car, an extension of the American's living room, followed the same pattern, as multiple speakers, FM, cassette players, and stereo were installed. Drivers use air conditioning, which helps seal the listener against outside intrusion, to transform the car into a concert hall—with the exception of teenagers, who want to escape the restrictions of being enclosed:

"What kind of sound equipment to you have in the car?"

"Six speakers, an equalizer, amplifier, tape deck, and tuner."

"What size speaker?"

"The system itself runs 80 watts."

"Do you have air conditioning?"

"I'm taking out the air conditioning."

"But the air conditioning allows you to drive with the window closed! You can hear the music!"

"Except I drive with the T-roof down. That's why I got so much power. You take out the sides, because when you drive on the highway you need to."

"Is the system for you or others?"

"Both for me and for other people. I use it to block out the rest of the world, as a way of being in my own state besides the rest of the world going on around me. I can deal with the world."

One portion of the population is using increasingly smaller and smaller units with excellent sound quality, and another portion is lugging around increasingly heavier portable sets (street furniture) with overpowering sound quality. A leading distributor of home electronic and sound equipment advertised the "Complete 'Take-Along' AM/FM Cassette System."

> This one does it all—play pre-recorded cassettes, tune AM, FM or FM stereo, and record tapes off-the-air "live" using the two built-in electret mikes. And with mike-mixing you can even "sing-along" during play-back. Seven function keys, including pause and cue-review, plus full Auto-Stop and LED indicator for "search" mode. Tape selector gives you optimum results with normal or CrO_2 cassettes. Separate volume, balance and tone controls, tape counter, and monitor switch for listen-ing while you record. LED display shows output power, recording level, and battery condition. LED FM stereo indicator. Jacks for external re-mote mikes, speakers, headphone. $10\frac{1}{2} \times 17\frac{1}{2} \times 5$". U.L. listed. AC operation or 8 "D" batteries (not inc.) or external DC power.

Everyone who buys large portable stereophonic cassette systems does not act out the same scenario or have the same motives. They are compact units which are handy for the student who wishes to have a system in the dormitory room, for the person who cannot afford the components of a quality stereo system. It can, however, be an act of imposition which is consciously practiced by someone willing to carry a heavy radio in public places. The weight of such a portable system is approximately twelve pounds, and the cost ranges from one hundred to three hundred dollars (a portable AM-FM transistorized radio can weigh less than a pound). The particular model described above is listed at around $220. Sales figures indicate that most AM/FM stereo cassette systems are purchased by teenagers, particularly blacks and Hispanics, and are generally referred to as simply "boxes" "monster boxes," "sub-way masters," or "jungle boxes," (the racial slur is obvious).

While portable radios have been in the public sector for thirty or forty years, the "box" has aroused particular public anger and provoked the enforcement of municipal statutes or the passing of new ordinances. Russell Baker wrote:

> One of the things poor kids in New York like to do is walk around carrying a big machine they call a "box." The box plays music through a radio and sometimes in the fancier models, through cassette machin-ery.
>
> It almost always plays this music very loudly. Sometimes you can hear the box coming a block or two away. It drives a lot of people crazy. These people say that the box makes noise, not music.

How you feel about this depends on your definition of music. If your idea of music is being hounded through the streets by the amplifiers from a rock concert in Madison Square Garden, if your idea of music is a subway collision followed by the screams of the injured, the box stuff is music. . . .

There is also the theory that the kid with a box is making a statement. Is there anybody who isn't making a statement these days?[1]

Since 1972 New York City has had a noise control code as part of its administrative code. Section 1403.3-4.03 states that "no person shall operate or use any radio, phonograph, or tape recorder in or on any rapid transit railroad, omnibus, or ferry in such a manner that the sound emanating from such reproduction device is audible to another person.[2] Another part of the statute covers radios played in other public places and specifies "unnecessary noise" as a violation.[3] In 1980 the police took action against acoustical pollution by confiscating radios played at too loud a public level. During May of that year fifty-nine summonses were issued for violations of the City's noise code, and twenty portable radios were confiscated. The radios would be returned to the owners upon payment of a twenty-five dollar fine. Thirty youngsters under the age of sixteen were issued "youth cards for alleged violations but were allowed to keep their 'boxes' because their age exempted them from normal court procedures and evidentiary requirements."[4] Enforcement focused on a specific segment of the population. The *New York Times* report indicates that city officials were taking the campaign seriously.

The authorities say that the campaign has just begun and point out that those summer months with the maximum auditory aggression are still ahead. They are hopeful that even a few confiscations of radios may have a large effect on a phenomenon that has caused increasing irritation to New Yorkers already beset by loud horns and sirens.[5]

Later figures show that a total of 236 summonses were issued in July and August of 1980 for radios that were played at too great a volume in the streets and in the subways. In contrast "the police are averaging 215 summonses a month for noisy vehicle mufflers, 125 for horn honking, and 158 for other unnecessary noise."[6] Noisy radios accounted for 24 percent of the summonses, a high proportion in an urban community beset by "loud horns and sirens"—an indication of the particular irritating effect of the "box" on the public.

In an age when there is great concern about the effects of television and film upon violence in our society, at a time when hostility often seems commonplace, it is to be noted that the concept of *auditory aggression* becomes the subject of police officials. It is noteworthy that a blaring radio is perceived as a hostile attack upon unwilling listeners.

The recognition of auditory aggression elevates a portion of acoustical pollution as a serious problem in urban society. In *The Tuning of the World,* R. Murray Schafer states that "when sound power is sufficient to create a large acoustic profile, we may speak of it, too, as imperialistic. For instance, a man with a loudspeaker is more imperialistic than one without because he can dominate more acoustic space."[7] The linking of territory and sound is central to understanding selective attitudes toward public sound in an urban context. Why do certain types of acoustical pollution become so much more irritating than other types? Why is the blaring radio more of a threat than the repetitive blasting of the car horn?

In *The Silent Language,* anthropologist Edward T. Hall says,

> Every living thing has a physical boundary that separates it from its external environment. Beginning with the bacteria and the simple cell and ending with man, every organism has a detectable limit which marks where it begins and ends. A short distance up the phylogenetic scale, however, another, non-physical boundary appears that exists outside the physical one. This new boundary is harder to delimit than the first, but it is just as real. We call this the "organism's territory." The act of laying claim to and defending a territory is termed territoriality.[8]

In *Sociobiology: The New Synthesis,* Edward O. Wilson defines "territory" as "an area occupied more or less exclusively by an animal or group of animals by means of repulsion through overt defense or advertisement."[9] Territoriality is part of human nature and is expressed in architecture, urban planning, in attitudes toward home, community, and possession. Territoriality crosses all classes and cultural lines, although it will be manifested in different ways. It is an overpowering force and an influence on the character of interaction occurring in any form of institutional life and shared environment.

Spatial relationships are among the countless variables which shape the particular ambience and quality of a place. In situations where people are crowded together, the individual is forced to adapt his or her sense of personal space. Everyone has been in situations where they felt uncomfortable when someone got too close to them under the circumstances of that specific occasion. A considerable amount of research literature is available on the study of personal space, or proxemics (the use of space as an aspect of culture), and nonverbal interaction. The space that exists around each individual is a complex facet of territory. Wilson refers to this relationship as "individual distance" or "social distance" and defines it as "the minimum distance that an animal routinely keeps between itself and other members of the same species." [10]

Many factors influence social distance, such as the specific cultural context and the individual's needs and desires. Generally, personal space ("personal space," "social distance," and "individual distance" are here used interchangeably) is described in visual terms. Space can be seen, it can be measured. There is a clear link between distance and the perception of appropriate vocalization.

> Not only is a vocal message qualified by the handling of distance, but the substance of a conversation can often demand special handling of space. There are certain things which are difficult to talk about unless one is within the proper conversational zone. [11]

Vocal decorum is related to social distance. When someone is very close to you, within 3 to 6 inches, the volume that would be expected would be a whisper. Public distance, which Edward Hall considers to be 5½ to 8 feet between the communicating individuals, demands "full voice with slight overloudness; public information for others to hear." [12] The intimate space of love requires the tender voice. Can you imagine love at a shout, or a sotto voce argument? The stereotype of the top sergeant standing nose to nose with the sad sack army trainee while screaming at him, dressing him down, is an example of personal space being manipulated and an act of verbal violence.

Personal space surrounding an individual, or between one person and another, is measured visually. Personal space is accompanied by acoustical space, which is generally expected to vary with the purpose of communication and the occasion. The appropriate level of vocal volume depends on the nature or type of interaction. Most of the time it is expected that acoustical and personal space be congruent.

The concept of acoustical space and its relation to territoriality is not new, although it seldom is linked to social distance. There are, however, auditory boundaries as well as spatial ones. Edward O. Wil-

son points out that many animals exhibit aggressive behavior to maintain their territory and that "repetitive vocal signaling" is one means
of accomplishing that task. "Familiar examples include some of the
more monotonous songs of crickets and other orthoperan insects. Such
vocalizing is not directed at individual intruders, but is broadcast as a
territorial advertisement."[13] Murray Schafer suggests that the genesis
of the concept is the territorial calls of birds.

> The definition of space by acoustic means is much more ancient than
> the establishment of property lines and fences; and as private property
> becomes increasingly threatened in the modern world, it may be the
> principles regulating the complex network of overlapping and interpen-
> etrating acoustic spaces as observed by birds and animals will again have
> greater significance for the human community.[14]

Schafer than provides several significant definitions.

> The acoustic space of a sounding object is that volume of space in
> which the sound can be heard. The maximum acoustic space inhabited
> by a man will be the area over which his voice can be heard. The
> acoustic space of a radio or a power saw will be the volume of space
> in which those sounds can be heard.[15]

Schafer reaches an important conclusion: "Modern technology has given
each individual the tools to activate more acoustic space."[16] It is not
surprising that portable stereophonic cassette systems equipped with
large powerful speakers are responded to with anger and police action.
Since each of us exists in both a personal and acoustical space, we are
violated when that space is invaded by an outsider who manipulates a
shared space with a turn of a knob. We are particularly offended when
it occurs in a confined, crowded space such as a bus, train, or subway,
where our personal and acoustical space has already been violated.

Subways, whether it be the Metro in Paris, the tube in London, or
the ornate system in Moscow, are fairly accurate indicators of life and
style in those metropolitan areas. Life on a New York subway is an
unpredictable and sometimes unpleasant adventure. Visually and
acoustically, the New York system appears to be a disaster area with
layers of graffiti hiding any remote sign of institutional paint and decor.
The metal wheels of outmoded cars screech into stations at an awesome decibel level harmful to the human ear. The response to the
visual and acoustical pollution is quite similar: the individual is impo-
tent, defenseless against personal violation. Russell Baker was correct,

someone is making a statement and it emerges (initially) out of the cries of the disenfranchised, from the young blacks and Hispanics who find themselves outside an upward striving society. Perhaps, now and then, there is an artistic dimension to the dense subway decoration and the rhythmic blaring, but generally the act of intrusion is a demonstration of hostility and an attempt to subject others to a tyranny which is from outside the social system—and which can be controlled. Acoustical invasion, like graffiti, is a demonstration of power and intimidation, and we are not in control.

Just imagine sitting in that subway car. It's not yet overly crowded with workers trying to get home. As people enter at each stop they try to locate themselves in their own tight little space, avoiding any contact (if it is made, it is fleetingly embarrassing) or interaction. Numerous private worlds exist within a public conveyance. Each form of public transportation imposes a set of conventions which are determined in large part by the physical structure of that mode. The decorum of public transportation allows for *some* body contact in a crowded vehicle, but the lack of eye contact appears to make body contact a mere illusion. The train thunders into the station, the doors slide apart, those trying to get on collide with those getting off: body contact, personal space, and acoustical space are not at issue, because getting on and off public conveyances renders all participants invisible for a short period of time (now and then someone objects to the pushing and shoving, but that person clearly does not understand the rules of the game). It is literally a period of limbo, "no-man's land," a transition between living spaces. This time, however, the ritual of the ride is disturbed by the entrance of an alien who is preceded by the unmistakable beat of reggae, disco, or rock. For a moment all heads turn to the source of invasion, but quickly the glances slide away, because the intruder dares anyone to look him in the eyes. He (the keeper of the machine is seldom a she) saunters down the aisle exuding confidence, arrogance, and smug hostility (a walk always accompanies the act). "I dare anyone here to ask me to shut off the music!" He finds a space, but does not sit in the usual sense. Rather he occupies a territory. His acoustical sphere of influence extends beyond his personal space. He relaxes and gets into the music—a dramatic gesture. He has established and publicly identified himself, and the rest of the car is dismissed until the next stop when the "subway master" decides to leave for new domains. The rest of the relieved riders settle back into their own protective cocoons as order and tranquility are restored with his departure. It isn't a very unique or creative act, but it is an effective gesture, because it intimidates, violates, and frightens the victim. Why?

It is the controlled use of power manifested in sound, gestures, and bodily stance. If the situation were changed a bit, what would the reaction be? Imagine the same subway car as a well-dressed man or woman enters with a "box" blasting Beethoven's Ninth Symphony. Is this intimidation? Is our reaction different? Are we now kindred spirits because Beethoven's Ninth is part of our world—a world we share? Would some sense of kinship be communicated to the keeper of the box, or have we still been violated because the protective acoustical bubble has been invaded? What happens if two subway masters find themselves in the same car? The ultimate duel of "monster box" versus "subway master"—the winner take all territory? In some prisons the "yard" is divided into the acoustical territories where each ethnic or racial group has a "box" and a box-master in charge.

The "box" is a means of achieving power. In that sense, the "box" and the motorcycle (as used by the Hell's Angels, for example) are related, because both use sound as power. It is tempting to suggest that there is a connection between the size of the instrument and the degree of perceived power one has within the culture. Therefore, the less social power you have, the larger the motorcycle or portable stereo system, and the louder the sound. It is, however, a provocative unproven thesis. The motive of those individuals who use the "box" in this public fashion can be guessed at, but it is debatable whether those in question would be able to articulate why they do what they do, even though it appears deliberate. The "box" helps establish territory, whether it is a subway car or a bus or the corner hang-out. The popular psychologist and columnist Dr. Joyce Brothers wrote in *High Fidelity Trade News* that the statement the "boom" box (another descriptive moniker) makes is "I can do what I wish, and it doesn't bother me what your reaction will be . . . I want to be taken seriously, even if it means being taken negatively. I want to be taken as counting, even if it's negative." [17] The amplitude of the "box" creates an acoustical space which can be increased or decreased simply by manipulating the volume control. Acoustical space is not dependent upon the user's physical size, either (as long as the person is strong enough to carry the system). The user is surrounded by a wide cone of sound which identifies and protects the person inside. As the volume is increased, as someone else's space is invaded, a degree of privacy is achieved by the box-master. No one wants to enter the cone of sound, because fear prohibits that action and because no one has enough natural decibel power to combat the volume. Portable public privacy is achieved by individuals who see themselves as alien to society (certainly estranged and connected to a subculture), discriminated against, and rejected. Portable public privacy is not only a display of arrogance, but also an expression of a particular vision of the world. That view of the world is instantly recognizable because the music is an indicator of both culture and style. Punk, disco, the variations of rock, heavy metal, country and western, etc., are identifying statements and expressions of attitude. For some, the "box" provides a relatively easy way to express deeply felt emotions nonverbally. It is not necessary to be articulate to express contempt, antagonism, and anger through a stereo cassette player.

Many of us surround and protect ourselves with walls of sound while we are engaged in public activity. A bicycle is adorned with a small radio. A picnic includes a portable radio in the spread. The distance between blankets on a crowded day at the beach is not only determined by personal space, but by zones of music. Dials are adjusted and speakers stationed in the right direction. And when we enter our cars and automatically turn on the radio we are assured that we are not alone and that we have protective company for as long as the journey lasts.

The wall of sound, that sense of acoustical space which surrounds each of us, is not always displayed by speakers blaring out sound. The wall of sound is often silent, nonpublic, not shared with others. In contrast with large portable stereophonic cassette units, the alternative of mini-portable stereophonic units has been developed for people who are mobile and wish to hear music privately. The spectator at the baseball game carries a mini-portable radio and an ear plug which provides the "play by play" broadcast. The jogger, the walker, the skier, and the roller skater can wear tiny headphones equipped with padded ear cushions. The office worker can listen to his or her own tunes without disturbing colleagues. The rest of the world can be shut out. "Walkman" (previously also called "Soundabout") was originally developed by the Sony Corporation in Japan for weary commuters who wanted relief from the boredom of their routine daily roundtrips. Ordinary radios would not work because of high tension wires and electrical interference. A Walkman provides a private stereophonic experience for *any* mobile individual, no matter where that person might be located. Such units also supply a second jack so that a pair of headphones can be connected so that the intimate musical experience can be shared with a chosen companion (a couple literally bound together by music). Additionally, some have a control and built-in microphone which converts the unit into an intercom system and allows for singing or conversing over and with the music.

Richard Warren of *The Chicago-Sun Times* described the unit as "the final solution to the punk problem. Require all the kids with those blaring boxes on the trains to trade them in for a Soundabout."[18] In *The New York Times* Hans Fantel said that the unit was ideal "for commuters traveling by train, giving them the same chance to sweeten their daily trek as is enjoyed by automobile travelers riding to the tunes of their car stereo."[19]

> Unlike the raucous boxes carried nowdays by indefatigable rock fans, it affords privacy both ways: Though heard at full volume by the listener, the music disturbs no one else. Conversely, the listener is sonically isolated and psychologically removed from his surroundings. Schubert on Conrail unquestionably helps in traversing the South [home of the "box"] Bronx.[20]

The mini-stereo-cassette unit is legitimized for the high economic class and contrasted with the "monster box." It's the thinking man's box and no one will be bothered!

> As astonishing as the fact that a pocket-size set plays true stereo sound with stereo separation is the fact that most of the people currently plugged into the unit on the city's streets look as if they wouldn't be caught dead lugging around those cumbersome portable radio "boxes."
>
> "I couldn't even lift one of those monstrous box things but I love this," said Karen Meyers, who was listening to "Pavarotti's Greatest Hits" on her Walkman as she strolled along East 57th Street. Miss Meyers said she had bought the set because "its sound is so fantastic and it shuts out the awful sound of the city."[21]

One of the stranger audio products merchandized with the feature of private sterephonic sound was the "Bone Fone" which wrapped around the shoulders of the user. The full page advertisement which appeared in *Roller Skating* is quite revealing about personal and acoustical territory.

You're standing in an open field. Suddenly there's music from all directions. Your bones resonate as if you're listening to beautiful stereo music in front of a powerful home stereo system.

But there's no radio in sight and nobody else hears what you do. It's an unbelievable experience that will send chills through your body when you first hear it.

AROUND YOU

And nobody will know you're listening to a stereo. The entire system is actually draped around you like a scarf and can be hidden under a jacket or worn over clothes.

The Bone Fone is actually an AM/FM stereo Multiplex radio with its speakers located near your ears. When you tune in a stereo station, you get the same stereo separation you'd expect from earphones but without the bulk and inconvenience. And you also get something you won't expect.

INNER EAR BONES

The sound will also resonate through your bones—all the way to the sensitive bones of your inner ear. It's like feeling the vibrations of a power stereo system or sitting in the first row listening to a symphony orchestra—it's breathtaking.

Now you can listen to beautiful stereo music everywhere—not just in your living room. Imagine walking your dog to beautiful stereo music or roller skating to a strong disco beat.

You can ride bicycle or motorcycle, jog, and even do headstands— The Bone Fone stereo brings beautiful music to every indoor activity without disturbing those around you and without anything covering your ears.

The rest of the advertisement deals with the invention of the product and provides a specific technical description. However, one additional paragraph is significant because of its reference to space:

YOUR OWN SPACE

Several people could be in a car, each tuned to his own program or bring the Bone Fone to a ball game for the play by play. Cyclists, joggers, roller skaters, sports fans, golfers, housewives, executives— everybody can find a use for the Bone Fone. It's a perfect gift.[22]

While the speakers of a portable radio or cassette player create a wall of amplified sound, earphones and earplugs create a silent wall, which separates the listener from those around him or her. The earphone mentality is based on privatization and isolation—on withdrawal from public sound and interaction. For some, like the roller skater or the music aficionado, excluding the extraneous helps them concentrate. For commuters, the motive is to create another sound environment, replacing the one which accompanies the mundane, routinized ritual, or to substitute pleasant sound for often harmful noise. Some jobs do not require thinking, because they have been absorbed into a routine of repetitive manual tasks. How many times have you commuted from home to work without remembering anything that occurred during the trip? People who drive are often not aware of the many manual operations they perform during the usual repetitive trip. Earphone listeners separate the sensory world transmitted into the cranium from the reality of mindless manual tasks. The sanitation or assembly line worker does not care to hear the sounds of the street or the factory; he or she prefers to escape them. The jogger is distracted from the pain of running or avoids the monotony of a daily route. In such situations the original sound source is separated from its new use and environment. Energy is directed inward, the visual images induced by the sound not congruent with the task at hand. The music triggers memories and fantasies, while muscle and motor coordination operate in the routine world.

One example of substituting a sound environment occurs frequently in the experience of air travellers. The airlines recognize the danger of boredom in long-distance travel. The passenger who is kept busy forgets the ordeal of travel. One pays to be plugged into the multichannel sound system. If you are unable to sleep on a plane, if your neighbor seems morose and uncommunicative (or if you wish to be morose and uncommunicative), if there is nothing you wish to read, the flight is long, and the scenery does not change. The desire to wander down the aisle and visit the pilot grows stronger, but the urge is suppressed by the watchful crew. Strapped in the middle of a six-person row, there is nothing to do but concentrate on the vibrating engines which sound a bit strange and fantasize the plunge downward and the moment of impact. Strapped to an unhealthy auditory and visual experience, one surrenders to the substitute two-dollar sound environment, along with earplugs that offer the additional sensation of pain (first-class passengers have the benefit of modern padded earphones and are robbed of the additional sensory experience). Unfortunately, the ear phones are only provided on relatively long flights where motion pictures are shown. If you don't want to see the movie or, more accurately, hear the movie, you have no choice but to accept a fate of boredom or attempt to sleep or arouse the anger of nearby passengers who are annoyed by the persistent glare of your reading lamp. Travellers who take shorter flights are doomed to the hallucinations induced by whining engines or to getting to know the person sitting next to them, although a forty-five minute shuttle is not conducive to airline romances or anything beyond the "how are you," "where are you from," "I have a friend in that town," stage.

Using earphones in public has another additional consequence, perhaps intentional at times, but often incidental in intent. The user is cut off from interaction with others. The airline passenger leaning back wearing earphones signals neighbors that conversation is not desired. The plugged-in commuter retreats into private sound. A colleague walks down the halls locked into an unknown world of music, precluding conversation with an unplugged scholar, which might have been equally stimulating and entertaining. The earphone/earplug prevents outside but often necessary sounds from entering awareness. One manufacturer has therefore produced a muting switch which temporarily turns down the volume when the conductor asks for a ticket or someone simply asks a question. The muting switch allows the questioner to reach you at half the decibel level. The person has your attention, but not *all* of it is granted. You maintain control of your sensory world.

The public earphone user creates a private world similar to that of the "box" user. Joyce Brothers considers the Walkman user more polite than the "boom box" culprit and suggests that the Walkman statement is "I am concerned about your reaction, but not all that concerned. I'm still in my own world." [23] Is the user of the Walkman more considerate than the master of the "monster box?" Each moves in a portable acoustical bubble, and while the effect of the miniaturized unit is less political than the box (certainly an important distinction), each of the users display some attempted mastery of his or her own moveable turf. The earphones establish an acoustical territory which is not to be entered without permission and which restricts interaction with outsiders. The wall of sound is silent, but communicates quite clearly. The presence of a Walkman renders the outsider invisible—a strange and unsettling feeling. It is equally strange to witness a person gyrating and foot-tapping to an imperceptible beat. The suspicion of a possible mental disturbance vanishes with the sight of an earphone, and the alien walks and jogs to the beat of a different tape.

THE PRIVATE MUSEUM

The imposition of a private sphere upon a public one also occurs in the phenomenon of self-guided museum tours. Instead of a museum tour guide, the visitor is supplied, for a slight fee, with a tape-recorded description of the exhibit. Two systems are in use. The first is essentially random: the museum-goer is supplied with an earpiece and enters separate transmission zones for each case of objects or work of art where a repeatable short message is played. The visitor can go to any part of the exhibit and wave a magic wand to activate a few words of explanation. The second, more regimented system provides a carefully developed discussion about a series of exhibits or works. The visitor is supplied with a cassette tape recorder, an orienting map, and an earphone. It is by far the most prevalent system. The leading producer of these tours is the Acoustiguide Corporation of New York and London. Such tours are not limited to museums, but are now being used in libraries, historical sites, for outdoor walking and auto-tours. Among the institutions which provide "Acoustiguide" tours of their permanent collections and/or special exhibitions are the Ägyptisches Museum, Berlin, the Fine Arts Museum of San Francisco, the Guggenheim Museum and Metropolitan Museum of Art in New York, and the Tate Gallery and the National Gallery of Victoria in London. Actually, most of the world's major museums have adopted such self-guided tours and therefore they no longer need to go to the expense of training docents, nor does their lecturing style have to disturb other visitors.

> Hello, I'm John Walsh, Curator of Painting here at the Museum of Fine Arts [Boston]. Along with Elizabeth Jones, Conservator of Paintings, I'm going to be your guide through our exhibition, "Monet Unveiled," a new look at Boston's paintings. Before we begin our tour, I'd like to say a few words about your Acoustiguide. The start-stop switch allows you to turn it off whenever you would like to linger with a painting we finished discussing or examine one that we don't have time to talk about. And you should definitely turn off your machine whenever you hear this signal [the listener hears a short mellow beep] for that means that the next painting is more than a step or two away and you should turn off your machine until you get there. Our tour begins in the gallery directly opposite the desk where you picked up your Acoustiguide, and I'd like you to walk in now and stop just inside the door and drink in your first impressions while I say a few general words about the exhibition.[24]

Certainly, the visitor, particularly the occasional patron for whom such a tour is really designed, will learn a great deal about the works of art being viewed and discussed. The taped tour lasts between 38 and 44 minutes and ten or more specified works are analyzed. There is an appeal to learning about art with the intimate charms of a cultivated expert personally whispering in your ear. However, the sight of intense and seriously committed visitors silently walking through the halls, mysteriously directed by an inner voice, is also somewhat disturbing. Art patrons stroll along in their acoustical bubbles under the gaze of uniformed guards who mutter into their walkie-talkies. The electronification of the museum indicates some philosophical shifts in regard to the "art experience."

The museum is being transformed from a social mileu, a dynamic environment in which people interact with art, decor, and *each other,* to an environment inhabited by individual inner-directed (and other-directed) art appreciators. The museum as event is de-emphasized as it becomes the place where art is displayed, explained, and appreciated. It is the place where the significance and history of art is carefully explicated. This well-ordered appreciation of a series of works is contrasted with the often disordered and complex experience of the architecture in which the works of art are housed, the ambience and sound which permeate the interior, the spectacle of other visitors— and (not forgotten) the aesthetic experience of the art works themselves. The museum experience is more than the meeting of person and object. Those who choose to take the taped tour share the common experience of the paintings or sculpture, but they do not share the museum as event or each other. . .

What is the ideal museum experience? Is it one where the public enters the domain with a sense of silent sanctity and awe—the efficient and orderly procession of persons sucking in culture? On the other hand, there is a philosophy that the museum is something more than a custodian of art and an educator of the masses, that the institution has a responsibility and relationship with the community, that it serves a social function. A mausoleum-like hush descends on an environment in which the wired museum visitors do not talk to each other, but are attentive to works of art. Obviously, the taped tour is not mandatory, and the proportion of visitors who participate can vary from five to fifty percent. Nevertheless, it is a significant development because it manifests a philosophy both of aesthetics and a museum's function. It is doubtful that the synthesis of the museum experience and sound technology will be reversed.

The tape-recorded tour offers advantages to both museum administrators and patrons. The tour can be offered in several languages. The visitor is not tied to a large group of stampeding people, but has the freedom to stroll alone. The quality of the tour will not vary according to the knowledge or style of the guides. The museum does not have to train guides, or administer the program.

People who engage an electronic tour guide react differently to the art experience than those who attempt the adventure without benefit of earphone guidance and brave the wilderness of art sans electronic instruction. Someone who is being privately instructed does not have to look at the title of the work to discover the subject matter or the name of the artist. The latter is an important part of the museum game played by the traditional patron. "Did I guess the artist?," or the "recognition game," is a measurement of personal artistic awareness on the part of the visitor. The recorded tour stresses precise information, not intuition, guess work, or misinformation. The unguided visitor drifts around the room until lured into contemplation. The recorded tour is, by definition, orderly and linear. The patron is gently led from work to work: the traffic pattern is predetermined.

It is difficult to defend the position that less information is better than more. There is, however, something about this method of transmitting information, not the knowledge itself, that clashes with the aesthetic experience. The sight of individuals concentrating upon an unseen guide's mellifluent voice is disturbing because the (ideal) meandering, contemplative appreciator has been replaced by the automated visitor intent upon education, led by mysterious forces lurking somewhere in the bowels of the museum. It is difficult to divorce the element of manipulation from the wired tour, yet, at the same time, the historical background, social commentary, critical dimension, and analysis of technique that the tapes provide must be recognized. The self-guided tour alters the nature of the museum experience, for better or for worse, depending upon one's point of view. What cannot be argued, however, is that the acoustical ambience of the museum is changed. The relationship between visitor, work of art, and fellow patrons is changed.

The kinship between patron and museum is important. The director or curator is used as narrator of a taped tour to establish a warm and intimate ambience. Ed Woodward of Acoustiguide explained, "we try to reflect the personality of the individual giving the tour, because what you are doing there is developing a one to one bond with the curator—a walk through the gallery with the curator—that is really the key."[25] The curator is an articulate and interesting person who intimately appreciates the particular works being displayed. The awareness of this bond is so important that the producers are hesitant to introduce other voices, even those of the contemporary artists themselves, commenting on their own works, or of other museum officials, discussing their design of particular exhibits.

> As soon as you introduce that second voice, you've provided a distracting device. So having attained this one-to-one relationship, you then take it away by having the artist come on and that is definitely a negative. That's why we try to avoid doing tours that have two voices for no good reason.[26]

Instead of stressing relationships that are shared among the visitors, a new one is established with the curator. The communication patterns of the earpiece people are quite significantly distinguished by an increase in nonverbal communication: hand gestures, shrugs, and eye contact between friends who share the experience of the guided tour, but hear only the voice of the guide in their individual earpiece. "Look at that" becomes a tap on the shoulder and a pointed finger. "Isn't that amazing!" is translated into a light push on the back toward a direction, lips puckered, eyebrows raised, and palm open with fingers extended. Those individuals, with benefit of the taped tour, tend to get more involved with each other, but clearly are barred from inter-acoustical communication. The taped tour bars the unexpected encounter or possible flirtations as acoustical segregation is surprisingly rigid. That confusing confrontation of wired and unwired patrons is a moment of embarrassment similar to the situation which occurs when a foreigner unable to speak English asks you for directions and you are unable to assist because you can't speak the language.

As long as choice is available the issue is not very serious. The institution of the docent has disappeared, probably because it was uneconomical and limited in the number of patrons that could be served, but it was the interaction of institutional personality with the public that transcended the mere enlightened contact between patron and art.

INSTITUTIONAL SOUND

While the merits of the self-guided tour can be argued, it is obvious that the phenomenon does not stimulate interaction and conversation. It is another example of how individuals attempt to achieve privacy in a public milieu. The pocket-sized stereo cassette players equipped with small earphones isolate the user from the aural environment. It is that person's choice to disconnect or reconnect. The "box" is also based upon the user's decision to envelop himself in sound, although, in this case, those who do not wish to participate have no choice and are antagonized by the imposition of sound and volume. In the case of institutional sound, there is seldom a choice.

Factories, offices, hotel lobbies, elevators, and the bathrooms of large hotels are filled with the soft sound of muzak. Restaurants and department stores add a musical decor in serving customers. The ubiquity of these sounds is the result of management decisions that the use of music will enhance an economic and/or psychological climate. Buyers, clients, employees, transient members of the public, are not offered the option of whether they desire a musical climate or not. Instead of acoustical space and the individual's welfare being the primary considerations, acoustical territoriality of the business establishment and productivity become the main issues. The walls of sound do not surround the individual, but rather delineate working/operating space and influence mood.

Institutional sound consists of two major categories: music used in the workplace and music provided in public places for people in transit or who find themselves in temporary locations. Institutional sound is unique because it is designed to be unobtrusive. The music should be heard, but must never be distracting. It is designed to be pleasantly innocuous. It is conspicuous when absent, but not consciously heard when present. It is never distracting and always assuring. There are a number of sources from which such music is available. In a very simple fashion, the output of a mellow-music radio station can be disseminated through the public communication system of a firm. There are also a number of companies which provide this kind of specialized service to their clients. MUZAK is probably the best known of such firms.

MUZAK began its operations in 1936 when it started transmitting music via telephone lines to hotels and restaurants. In 1980 the company was transmitting its programming to a daily listening audience claimed to be around 80 million people via a communications satellite. A spokesperson for MUZAK pointed out that the basic concept is to provide music which is part of the total environment. "We take a musical selection and re-arrange it, and re-record it with different in-strumentations and different styles so that it does not intrude. You can work with it and can converse with it without interrupting your con-centration."[27] Music supplies an aural environment and is part of the decor which characterizes a business establishment. Sound used in this way has three basic (not mutually exclusive) functions: to establish the appropriate mood and decor; to cut down on noise and distractions; and to increase productivity. However, the use of music to establish environment is indicative of a general attitude toward silence. Ob-viously, uncontrolled noise can be distracting, counterproductive, and even psychologically and physically harmful. But the presence of silence is seen as an equal, perhaps even greater menace. The spokesperson for MUZAK stated, "we maintain that most people are uneasy with an absence of sound. We feel an empty space requires some kind of pleas-ant sound. Music is one of the more pleasant sounds."[28] It is also pointed out that some noises are accentuated and startling if they occur within relatively silent environments. But there are few places which are truly silent, except those created by twentieth century technology. Part of the problem was created by modern office buildings which seal out all extraneous noise, creating a relatively silent environment which is unnatural and annoying. A need for a substitute auditory environ-ment has been created. The elimination of natural acoustical ambience is solved by the presence of a musical background. Relative silence can present a threat. For example, when you go into an empty public area that is usually full of activity, you feel a little bit uneasy. What is more haunting than standing on the stage of an empty theatre or being in a large office space late at night? There is uncertainty hidden in the unknown. The unexpected leaps out of silence. It is not part of the desired human experience to exist in silence. In those situations we produce our own human sounds to reassure ourselves. We accompany our fears with words muttered under the breath, a whistled or hummed tune, a nervous cough.

Silence ought not be confused with quiet. The contemporary indi-vidual grows up surrounded by music produced through ubiquitous loudspeakers. Are there places where one expects to meet a quiet at-mosphere, where the presence of music would be inappropriate? It is hard to think of such a place. The funeral parlor? No! One cannot bear the thought of death without pastel music filtering through the air. In a house of worship? Very seldom. The choir or the organ even provides background to prayer. Most people, and there are, of course, exceptions, sleep without music, but make sure that they fall asleep or awaken to the music of the clock radio. This culture has been programmed and weaned on a musical environment. When there is an absence of voice and/or natural sound in an enclosed place, we feel disconnected, disoriented, and desire music to re-establish a complete environment.

On the other hand, the presence of noise is considered undesirable. The shrill sounds of sirens, the hammering of pneumatic drills, the clatter of typewriters, the hissing of steam, and the screeching of machinery can be harmful and is certainly counterproductive. It is, therefore, desirable to eliminate noise whenever possible. Many companies are aware of their noise problems and solve the situation in different ways. When the landscape concept of office design became popular in the late 1950's, when management began to remove office walls to create an open working space for employees, both benefits and problems accrued. The new arrangement was seen as a means to improve communications and the flow of paper. In addition, it offered different design possibilities.

> Today, two of the most persuasive reasons for going open plan are the ease of rearranging office and the much lower cost of accomplishing this, compared with moving fixed partitions—perhaps 60 cents per square foot, versus 5 to 6 dollars.[29]

But the number of potential distractions also increased. Telephone conversations, calculators, typewriters, and general office noise have to be muffled as much as possible. Acoustical privacy in the open-plan office was recognized as economically important for the welfare of the concern. Ways of decreasing general background noise in such an office and at the same time providing an acoustical territory for each employee included using screens to redirect and absorb sound, treated ceilings, and masking devices. One such masking device is a white noise generator which produces a low almost imperceptible level of sound that masks other noises. While it is effective, the sound of the white noise generator, reportedly like an air conditioner, is constant and irritating with no variation in pitch or intensity. Therefore, many companies seeking some means of masking noise began to look for an alternative. One solution which MUZAK developed was a sound generator tuned to the ambience level of the particular environment. Selective frequencies match or combat the frequencies in a specific area and music is then superimposed over the masking frequencies. Apparently, the selective use of the sound generator achieves such acoustical privacy that a telephone conversation ten feet away is unintelligible. The sounds can be heard, but not understood. The intentions of the employer are positive in the sense that a better and efficient working climate is created for the employee. One wonders, however, if employees are informed when either white noise or sound generators are utilized. What are the employees' rights in regard to acoustical self-determination?

The economic welfare of the particular company and its productivity is paramount to its management. In that sense worker morale is a major factor since it is linked to economic success and failure. In order to combat monotony and offset boredom, and since individual radios (portable or the Walkman type) might present some chaotic problems, a very carefully arranged selection of music can be provided in which each quarter hour is programmed. MUZAK calls this programming "Stimulus Progression." Very simply, it assumes that during the course of a working day an employee's attention, concentration, vigor, and enthusiasm will vary. For example, at 10:30 in the morning the worker is less alert than at the beginning of the shift or just before the lunch break. Therefore, that dip can be countered by a change of beat and/or orchestration at that point. The slump is countered with an injection of up-beat musical energy. Productivity figures do indicate a positive change with this type of programming. There is to be found, for instance, a reduction of errors by typists and a decrease in the number of assembly line rejects. The MUZAK literature states:

> Experiments performed by the Human Engineering Laboratory of the U.S. Army in Aberdeen Proving Ground, Maryland, found that programmed functional music improves human vigilance, mental alertness, working efficiency. This applies particularly to routine or repetitive assignments.[30]

Among the companies that use both the masking device and muzak are the Xerox Corporation, United Parcel Service, the Telephone Company of Connecticut, the Young and Rubicam advertising agency, and Nissan Motors in Japan. The system works because it supplies or creates an audio environment which some find pleasant, it decreases irksome noise, and it aids in raising the efficiency of the employees. There are, however, some questions to be asked.

Does the employee have a choice? Is the worker informed in the job interview that he or she will be subjected to muzak for the entire working day? Or is it to be considered merely part of the decor over which the employee has few rights, if any? What are the psychological effects of being bathed in music during an entire working day? Obviously, once the person has been hired, choice is eliminated and control of the musical environment is in the hands of the executive in charge. One of the badges of the executive's authority is the control of his or her own acoustical environment. However non-executives are subject to musical manipulation.

The walls of sound which surround us, whether freely chosen or imposed by others, whether seen as beneficial or harmful, are part of our daily existence. In a democratic society each citizen has acquired certain inalienable rights to which might now be added the control of acoustical space, a right now temporarily abrogated. Acoustical space can be enlarged or decreased. It interacts with other individuals' respective acoustical spaces in a dynamic and often subtle process which is unconsciously and constantly adjusted as the environment and relationships change. The possibility for the constant control, by choice or imposition, of one's acoustical environment through electronic sound technology is now a reality. Social distance and acoustical space become asynchronous, become disconnected. In a society in which quiet is dismissed in favor of musical connection and connection subordinates human interaction, how do we deal with a human being who is spatially near us, but acoustically some place else? What happens to our attitudes toward sound and noise (one person's sound might be another person's noise) that are not managed, that are unpredictable?

Five

The Perception of Perfection

Why are we so fascinated by the tightrope act, the lion tamer, or the flying trapeze artist? Is it the beauty and grace of movement? Is it a matter of the odds and the chances for actual or artistic survival? Certainly, danger and uncertainty are attractions. The spectator's appreciation of a risky or dangerous act involves some contradictory emotional responses. We require that the potential for calamity be present, to a frightening imaginary degree, although the calamity is not desired— certainly not consciously. That imagined disastrous moment must, however, occur to someone sometime to underscore that "the daring young man on the flying trapeze" is truly "daring." The potential of tragedy, of disaster, of failure, underscores and defines success. The clever performer builds that tension into the act by introducing planned moments of uncertainty: the precarious wobble, the lunge for the safety of the platform, the dangerous mistake: all are aimed to produce a gasp from the audience. This intimate relationship between failure and success is not limited to spectacular performances of physical display, danger, and courage. It is a principle which applies to all the arts. The rendering of one composition is exceptional, the other merely adequate. Why?

There is something hypnotically compelling about the individual who dares to thrill an audience with eloquence or with a display of extraordinary dexterity. The magic of the performer-audience encounter involves a fascination and an appreciation of performance. It is an awe limited to live performances, which are not packaged encounters and the outcomes of which are never predictable. Physical presence is not quite as important as the liveness of the event—the sense that it is happening right now! The fallibility of that performance indicates its real appeal: *Something can go wrong.* The possibility of a mistake or error always lurks over the performance. Indeed, the extraordinary performance rests on a precarious tightrope where a slight error in judgment results in either artistic or physical failure. The dull performer does not take a chance; neither does the display of prosaic talent ever approach the daring of the extraordinary.

Basic ability is necessary, of course, before the excitement of chance plays a role. Lack of talent never thrills anyone. What distinguishes a performance during which the audience sits quietly bored from a performance where they are electrified and react to the "magic in the air?" It is quickly recognized when an actor goes beyond the ordinary and wanders into the shadowy domain where greatness and failure are fraternal. That tension between audience and performer suddenly propels a singer into a fearful display of vocal pyrotechnics. That moment is recognized when it occurs, because the audience physically and emotionally shares the moment.

The relationship between performer and audience has been altered by the media of communication and the technology of recording. For most people, contact with music today is primarily through the media of communication and therefore generally occurs after the actual performance. This is particularly true of contemporary music, in which the recording plays such an overwhelming role that the professional musician is absolutely dependent upon it for success. What are the ramifications of recording technology upon attitudes toward musical performance? What are the aesthetic criteria applied to a concert, and what are one's expectations in listening to an audio cassette recording, a phonograph record, or a digital laser disc of a musical performance? The technology of recording has changed the relationship between spectator, performer, and event.

One of the changes that the recording has introduced is the pressure for success the performer feels in committing his or her utterance or interpretation to some form of *permanent* preservation. No performer wishes to make permanent a moment of indecision or a wrong note. An ephemeral mistake is soon forgotten, but a recorded one remains a monument to failure. So it is not a surprise that the technology of sound recording has developed two primary goals. The first is to *faithfully* reproduce the sounds of musical performance and to transfer that experience to the environment of one's choice: living room, bedroom, or automobile. One measure of success, therefore, is to see how closely that performance can be technically duplicated. The second goal is to produce the quintessential realization of a particular work as performed by a specific musician or group of musicians. This raises a particularly interesting question: what is the expectation of the composer who creates with an ideal rendering in mind but whose work, unless it is totally synthesized or electronic, requires the interpretation of fallible performers?

Today, the medium of music is the recording. The music critic Henry Pleasants has stated that "where music was once propagated locally by the individual it is now propagated generally by the phonograph record, the radio, and the motion picture sound track."[1] Immanual Wilheim, Professor of Music at Hart College, points out that the listener's first musical experience, after the lullaby, is with a record rather than with a human performer. The effect is that the public has become accustomed to a "disembodied perfect sound."[2] Today, the greatest proportion of musical contact is not with the performer, but with the sound of music.

The development of sound technology has been relatively swift, and the impact has kept pace with the accelerating developments. Consider that Thomas Alva Edison received a patent for the phonograph in 1878, that the $33\frac{1}{3}$ rpm long-playing record was introduced by Columbia Records in 1948, and that the first commercial stereophonic discs were not introduced until 1958. Each step in technological sophistication resulted in more and more technical control over the recording process. The shift from directly recording on discs to using tape as an intermediate step in recording has had immense implications because it has so enhanced the potential to control and manipulate all elements. The tape recorder has brought about a psychological transition from an appreciation of recorded "real time" to the acceptance of "reel time."[3] The magic of "real time" was the possibility of hearing everything that occurred at the live performance transferred to the home through a disc with grooves which contained information that could be transformed into music. The recording and the institution which produced the recording were regarded as a proxy for the absent audience at the concert. Before 1948 it was assumed that a musician played for x number of minutes, that there was a one-to-one ratio of recording and playback performance.

> Before 1947 (the tape recording or "magnetophone," was invented in pre-war Germany), a recording session consisted of trying to capture a perfect performance. If the musician didn't achieve perfection then he had to start over again, because the sound was transcribed directly onto a wax master disc,[4]

So the listener's aesthetic and critical attitude was based upon the expectation that *the performance* would be replicated. The goal of "real time" replication is, however, eliminated, certainly deemphasized, with the perfection of tape. Today there are some rare attempts to create anachronistic "live tape recordings"—as opposed to what? The live performance is a real-time event, whereas the recording which uses tape as an intermediate facilitating agent has little relationship to real time. The tape-facilitated recording of particular length might merely represent a minute fraction of real-time performance.

The current technological shift in the recording industry from "analogue" to "digital" recording techniques has increased control still more.

> In a conventional recording, the sound from the musicians is picked up by a microphone, converted into an electrical signal and sent via the recording console to the tape recorder, which converts the electrical signal into a magnetic one recorded on the tape. As the musicians play louder, the signal from the microphone increases, as does the magnetic signal recorded on the tape. This directly proportional (or analogous) relationship of the music's loudness to the magnetic signal is the source of the term "analogous" recording.
>
> In a digital recording, microphones and recording consoles are also used, but here the signal from the recording console is sent to an analogue-to-digital converter. The A/D takes the analogue signal, chops it into pieces (sampling), assigns a number to each piece (quantization) and then converts each number into a binary form (BIT), a numbering system based on the powers of 2 which allows any number to be ex-

pressed by a series of 1's and 0's. Up to 50,000 samples per second can be taken with the best professional digital equipment with each sample converted into one of 2^{16} (or 65,536) quantized level.

Once in binary form, the signal can be stored by any method that can record 1's and 0's, the most convenient being magnetic disc, PCM (video) disc, photographic film, pure electronic methods or even punch cards could be used.

On playback, the digital signal from the tape (or whatever) is fed to a digital-to-analogue converter that reconstructs the original levels from data stream and then filters the "rough edges" off the signal to return it to an exact replica of the original signal.[5]

While the technology of digital recording has not been completely perfected (at this point the introduction of the digital player into the home lags behind the use of the system in editing recorded performances), in theory, "while in digital form, the recorded signal can . . . be copied an infinite number of times and then still be used to construct a 'perfect' audio signal."[6]

The recording of twenty-four separate audio tracks on a two-inch-wide piece of magnetic tape permits either the simultaneous recording of those tracks or sequential recording, that is, one element recorded after the other on separate tracks. Most popular music recordings utilize the overdubbing process in which individual elements of the composition or performance are built and combined, layer upon layer, until eventually a blend of all elements is synthesized. This system allows a singer, for example, to sing over a previously recorded musical accompaniment or even to sing over his or her own previously recorded vocal rendering.

To record a concerto, each movement is played one or more times and then sections in each movement are recorded numerous times, with specific "takes" recorded of any small section in which there might be some interpretative or technical problem. A recording session I witnessed of Bela Bartok's *First Piano and Violin Sonata* played by Pinchas Zuckerman and Marc Neikrug took place over a two-day period. To produce a recording of a sonata which takes approximately twenty-four minutes to perform, approximately six hours of music was recorded. The first movement was recorded on the first day. On the second day, the third movement was played first and then the second. Each movement was further broken down into inserts and multiple takes. All was recorded through seven microphones and a digital audio processor plus a regular audio recorder whose tape would be used as a reference for later editing—which would occur weeks or months later. Every mistake, each discernible flaw of artistic execution, any lapse in interpretation, is covered by a back-up series of recorded sections from which the errorless performance can be assembled—with the help of the sound engineer's technical virtuosity and his or her impressive paraphernalia. It is a meticulous process so exact that individual notes can be removed from the recording and replaced by preferred ones.

The recording of popular music is a somewhat different process, but is equally demanding and exacting. The track sheets prepared by guitarist Gordon Titcomb for the production of a "Country and Western" number called "The Queen of Spoons" show that nineteen of twenty-four available tracks were used. Of the nineteen tracks, twelve were originally and simultaneously recorded: two different bass channels, a vocal, an electric guitar, an original pedal steel part, piano (left and right for the stereophonic effect), acoustic guitar, and four channels of drums. Two complete takes were first recorded. The remaining seven tracks included an electric guitar, chorus, fiddle, spoons, background vocal I and background vocal II. The last two tracks were recorded right after each other, and the voices on them were electronically doubled using a "harmonizer." Where two people performed during each take, four voices were now heard. "If I just use a straight digital delay and delay it a little bit, the second voice which is a copy of the first will follow at an exact rate." [7] At the same time, to avoid the mechanical impression of absolute exactness, random variation is built into the machine.

> Such perfection makes us a little bit nervous. We don't want to hear notes mathematically correct. This machine can be programmed so that it can be off a human amount—a random amount. You can set how many milliseconds it can be off on either side of the beat—and it will be randomly off. The most amazing thing about it is what it is trying to do—to be an effect which is not an effect. It's trying to be an effect which sounds like human error. [8]

The remaining seven tracks, including the doubled voices, are slowly added to the original twelve tracks. Probably sixty to seventy hours are spent in recording three songs, and an equal amount of time is required for the mixing process. What is apparent in the recording of both classical and popular music is the degree of precision and detail that is required. This meticulous control creates numerous production options.

The possible variations in creating the final version are limitless. A recording is not merely a record.

To understand audio technology's impact upon the perception of music, some distinction has to be made between types of recordings and their relation to performance.

A *"live" recording* is the record of a performance. It is essentially a facsimile. What is stressed is replicating a musical event, which has been captured in its entirety, without interfering with the original performance. Even this simple development would alter the lives of professional musicians and the attitudes of the audience. In 1929 the late piano virtuoso Artur Schnabel was asked to make some recordings, but he was concerned with the undertaking.

> Until then I had consistently refused to do so. One of the chief reasons for my refusal was that I did not like the idea of having no control over the behavior of the people who listen to music which I performed— not knowing how they would be dressed, what else they would be doing at the same time, how much they would listen. Also I felt that recordings are against the very nature of performance, for the nature of performance is to happen but once, to be absolutely ephemeral and unrepeatable. I do not think there could even have been two performances of the same piece by the same person which were absolutely alike, that is inconceivable.[9]

Schnabel's arguments against recording seem alien today when replication has become so ingrained in our expectations. Of particular interest is Schnabel's point about "control," which has been transferred from the artist to the recording engineer.

Theoretically, the live recording attempts to recreate the basic performer-audience relationship. If only it were that simple! While a definition of performance might be agreed on, it is difficult to agree on a definition of a "live recording." It can be a recording of a performance given before an audience or of a performance without an audience. The appeal to the record-buyers is that they are purchasing the replication of an uninterrupted performance. On the other hand, the recording might consist of several different numbers performed at different locations and then assembled into one album. Note the following technical liner notes from Joan Baez's album "From Every Stage."

> The performances embodied in this recording were selected from concerts by Joan Baez in July and August of 1975. The artistic goal underlying the production of the album was to faithfully recreate the music

as it was experienced by the audiences at these concerts. There were no vocal overdubs whatsoever. The basic tracks were not enhanced or altered in any way. Great attention was given to placing instruments in the point of the stereo spectrum that would most accurately represent the positions of the musicians on stage. The primary effort achieved in the remix stage, then, was to make the recording as natural as the original performances.[10]

Is it possible to "faithfully create the music as it was experienced by the audience at those concerts?" The idea is intriguing, because it implies a philosophy of sound reproduction that is embraced by the artist and recording production team. What is the nature of the musical experience being created for the listener? Is the listener taken to the concert or does the concert come to the listener? Where are you when you listen to music? Are you always in the same place or does the musical distance vary from record to record? The number of microphones used, their placement, and the number of tracks used to record the music alters the sound that the consumer finally hears. According to Ed Woodard of Acoustiguide and Executive Vice President and Director of Marketing for Dahlquist Speakers, the "audiogenic designer," referring to engineers, A&R people, musicians, recording directors, and/or producers who construct sound images of sonic events, exercise a style through the control of "plausibility."[11] According to Woodard, "plausibility determines that point in time/space at which the listener positions himself or herself in the course of experiencing the listening event. That point is the locus of perception."[12] That locus can differ from recording to recording even though each circumstance might involve a live performance. When we perceive that the sounds we are listening to in a specific environment, perhaps the living room, could conceivably be produced in that very same environment, we are dealing with a "plausible sensation perceived in a plausible place." When, however, we perceive a plausible sensation in an environment which makes the reception somewhat implausible, we are transported to the concert hall or the event. Most of us cannot host a 100 piece orchestra in our living room. Woodard suggests that an impressionistic recording involves a plausible sensation in an implausible place. The point is that the relationship to the live/recorded performance is not as simple as one would first think, and the assumption that the live recording is merely a substitute for attending the actual event itself is rather naive.

The *"studio" recording* is an entity in its own right and is not restricted or defined by what might happen in a live performance, since the live performance is not the model by which this recorded event is to be judged. The recordings found within this category use audio technology as an additional musical instrument, and the results are performances which *are not possible* under normal live circumstances. No one is capable of singing a duet with oneself unless it is to accompany a previously tape-recorded solo, but a band of one is a distinct possibility when the full capabilities of the recording studio are available. Apparently Jascha Heifetz did once make a recording of the "Bach Double Violin Concerto" in which he played both of the solo parts. The Beatles' "Sgt. Pepper's Lonely Hearts Club Band" is an example of a marvelously inventive work which depended on the studio to create effects which would not be possible during an actual performance. Such a recording does not pretend to be anything other than what it is—a studio-produced work of art. The reference is not the performance. In that respect, the performer-audience relationship is unique because it is defined by the absence of actual confrontation—and the impossibility of that ever happening. The locus of perception for recordings of this ilk are therefore quite idiosyncratic. The sounds heard in the living room (or any other environment) are not attributed to any particular source or location. It does not matter where the actual recording session took place, because place is not relevant to this listening experience. Woodard considers such recordings expressionistic: recordings which consist of implausible sound sensations occurring in a non-existent place. "The locus of perception can then, logically only be found *within the listener.*" [13]

The *"live augmented" recording* uses studio facilities to enhance a basically live performance. The artist and producer seek to create the best possible recording in terms of quality of performance and audio fidelity. This is achieved through multiple-track recording, many takes, and electronic enhancement, but the primary purpose is to refine the original performance by the artist. With the aid of electronic technology this type of recording facilitates the errorless performance which is the goal of any artist. It is also possible to achieve a technically superior recording of an artistically inferior performance, which is frequently done. Some critics will evaluate the recording and the performance separately, although there are areas where it would be difficult to distinguish one from the other.

One of the problems in categorizing recordings on the basis of the relationship of the performer to the technology is the difficulty of distinguishing the presence of that technology. Is it to be assumed that all recordings are edited? Joan Peyser, former editor of *Musical Quarterly* assumes that all recordings *have been edited* unless a public denial is issued with the recording.[14] What the average person believes is another issue (or does it even matter?), since there is generally no information available with the album or cassette about the degree of editing that has taken place (Sixteen percent of this performance has been edited!). Should the public be informed? Some recordings are obviously "studio" recordings, and the nature of the sound is immediately recognizable as the product of the studio's engineering magic. For example, a vocal track with heavy reverberation or echo added is automatically processed by the listener with the understanding that something has been added to the human performance. No one can sing naturally in echo! The problems arise when one is unable to distinguish the presence of the studio in recordings which are assumed to be "live": a replication of a live performance which is aesthetically and critically appraised with the "live" model governing that experience.

In classical music, the "in-concert" recording has become common, perhaps with the goal of creating an unadulterated musical experience for the listener which is more authentic than in most recordings. In "The Trouble With Recordings," Joseph Horowitz quotes John Pfeiffer, a record producer who worked with pianist Vladimir Horowitz for many years:

> It is true that all these in-concerts recordings are edited, but this isn't the type of sewing machine work that you do with a lot of studio recordings—a few bars from this take, a few bars from another take, until you build up a master. There's always one overall performance that Horowitz prefers, but which includes certain things that have to be corrected. In the case of the Rachmaninov Third, for example, we remade literally everything that went wrong with the actual performance—a good two hours of music. But I didn't use more than, at most, ten minutes from the whole remake session.[15]

While the motive and zeal to correct mistakes is understandable, the ethical and critical issues are difficult ones. If recordings are going to be judged on the basis of perfection, the criteria and definition of perfection need to be articulated, a task which probably is impossible. But how is the artist's effort to be evaluated if one does not know how much of the performance was achieved technologically? Apparently very few recordings replicate a concert without some editing: how much is difficult to determine, and how much one would tolerate as acceptable depends on one's conception of purity.

The problem would not exist if recordings weren't compared with performances, but were considered performances in their own right. Composer/conductor Morton Gould addressed that issue:

> If you can come up with a dazzling interpretation of a Chopin etude, note perfect, letter perfect, with an impressive type of interpretation, even though this might be put together from a number of different takes, if it has the quality of inevitability, that's valid. I think the recorded performance is its own kind of performance.[16]

Morton Gould maintains that the comparison of a recording with a live performance is anachronistic. "Once you accept that, you accept the morality of the recorded performance."[17] But this denies the true impact of the recording on musical attitudes and tastes, because the live performance, with the exception of those studio productions which are impossible to create in live performance, is inexorably tied to the recording.

The live concert was, at one time, the stimulus for record sales. "That was great. Has it been recorded? Good, let's get a copy." The concert was the criterion by which the recording was judged. It served to remind the listener of a previous musical moment. "It's almost as if I were there. I can remember that evening." The recording was a means to recapture a sparkling and emotional moment shared with the performer and audience. Today the live concert is judged by the standards recording has established. More people listen to recordings than attend live concerts—popular or classical. If, however, a person does go to a concert, it is often because of a recording. "The record was fantastic. Let's go see him in person." The comparative judgment of the event is built into the experience. How can anyone avoid the natural tendency to compare the event with the recording? The audience is happy because the artist has come up to the expectations set by the recording, or they are unhappy because the performer has not lived up to the virtuosity displayed on the disc. Certainly, the acoustics of the hall did not match up favorably with the quality of the living-room stereophonic system or the tiny cassette player. In all probability, however, the recording has been altered and enhanced by studio engineering and production. A person, unaware of the influence of technological enhancement, evaluates the live performance (nonrecorded) with ideal standards. But even those who are aware of the distinction between the recording and performance will be influenced by the familiar recording. How is the comparison to be avoided? It should be noted that in response to the concert goers' expectations, the electro-acoustic concert hall has been created that can selectively accomodate the hall to the type of ensemble performing.

Critic Joseph Horowitz maintains that the studio performance cleansed of error is antiseptic compared with the more passionate concert performance.

> Vladimir Ashkenazy's in-concert recording of Chopin's B-flat Minor Sonata . . . the best Ashkenazy recording I know, is more stirring where he is least accurate: the final reprise of the scherzo, in which the cumulative thrust of the pounding, leaping octaves derails his fingers once or twice. Rachmaninov's unsurpassed recordings of the same work . . . also contain wrong notes in the scherzo.
>
> The wrong notes in the *Pictures* recording signify not technical inadequacy, but a sustained abandon rarely encountered in the studio. "The Hut On Fowl's Legs" is riddled with awkward octaves and precarious skips. There is probably no way to get all the notes right without applying an irrelevant degree of caution, yet this is what current studio practice demands.[18]

It is not the presence of error which makes those recordings exciting. It is the transcending experience shared by the listener with the performer which makes the moment so exhilarating. The recorded musical event is well served by high technical standards and freedom from errors of execution. The standard or ideal for the musical event, free of error, resides in the mind of the composer, and the score that results from that inspiration. But the performance is another matter, and the model must always involve the unpredictable, spontaneous result of the performing artist interpreting a work before an anticipating audience.

If the performer is talented, technically proficient, and is in addition inspired by the gods, he or she might almost reach the level which is achieved every day in the recording studio—a level of performance which need not, and should not, tolerate mistakes. There is no room for a mistake in a world where perfection can be manufactured—why should there be? If that slightly off-pitch note can be fixed, why allow it into the home where it reflects upon artist, composer, and producing company? The struggle of an artist to enter the realm of perfectibility is awesome compared to the ease with which the studio engineer can change, substitute, or manufacture notes, passages, and sections. Recording studio personnel can take a basic performance and perfect it, as long as the artist has provided a fundamental level of competence. But the electricity of a great live performance cannot be manufactured and furthermore requires a milieu in which the non-perfect, potential failure and success exist side by side. When we attend a performance we witness a struggle between an individual's artistic vision and the ability of that person to execute the composer's creation, which is intended to affect us emotionally and spiritually. It is the clash, the combat, which is of the essence in a performance. The musical experience is part of that struggle. The recording presents the musical experience without the combat. It is a rare moment when the performer succeeds in getting close to the goal of musical apotheosis and a "great" performance is witnessed—a rare event! It is never merely heard, but always seen and heard!

The two processes, the musical event and the performance event, influence and compete with each other. The existence of the definitive recording suggests that there is a perfect rendition against which people measure their experience in the concert hall. An audience accustomed to the perfect have no patience for the fallible performer who walks an artistic tightrope—not when the standard of performance is so easily obtained by turning on the radio or the turntable. The perfect is accessible, guaranteed, and repeatable. There is no way of assuring that the concert event will not be flawed by error or lack of inspiration, perhaps by disaster, and at a price of admission usually considerably higher than the price of the recording. Going to the performance means taking a chance. The effect of recordings upon the concert hall, for both classical and popular music, has been extraordinary. Joseph Horowitz described his reaction to a concert he attended several years ago at Carnegie Hall where Sir George Solti conducted the Chicago Symphony Orchestra in Brahms's First Symphony. While the audience was impressed by the great sound the orchestra created, Horowitz questioned the performance and later wrote that "an electronically dissected orchestra fed through giant speakers might have stirred up the same kind of excitement."[19] Horowitz claims that one of the reasons Solti and the Chicago Symphony are so well received is Solti's ability to "realistically emulate a recording in concert."[20] It should not be surprising that such excesses in sonority should develop, because the sound of the orchestra in a living room can be more overpowering than that sound experienced in the concert hall or arena. The recording has managed to change the sound of the live performance. Immanual Wilheim explains:

> We have become much more, as the result of electronics, ready to expect a certain deep reverberance, a brilliance in the upper registers, which can be artificially simulated by the recording engineer. That, in turn, creates in the audience, perhaps unconsciously in the musician too, a desire to hear in the concert hall something that originally was much more the creation of the recording engineer.[21]

Musical expectations and tastes are changing. Morton Gould's comments are quite revealing in regard to this trend:

> Aaron Copland's "Appalachian Spring" always sounds tremendously effective in the concert hall. I think of the very striking effect where the violins suddenly cascade up and down. And then I heard a recording of it and the recording made this section so much more present that when you heard it in the concert hall again, it sounded like the violins were set back in the texture of the orchestra.[22]

Does Morton Gould, as a conductor, therefore change his interpretation of "Appalachian Spring" the next time he conducts?

One of the things that has changed the sound of popular music has been the transformation of the musical instruments from acoustic to electronic. Today, the electronic instrument is a part of the standard live performance. Guitarist Gordon Titcomb explains:

> The Fender reverb amplifier was the standard of the industry for a long time for guitar players. It was a good amplifier with a hundred watts of power. It has reverb, a hammond spring, and three types of really archaic equalization boost. And that is just not enough now to get the sound you want to get. *You want sound as good as the record.* You want to be able to go in and not disappoint the people who bought the record. You want to be able to sound that good.
>
> The amplifier I just got has six bands of equalization. It has a phase shifter, which ten years ago was an incredibly expensive studio effect. Now you can buy just the unit itself—a phase shifter in which you put a nine volt battery. It's about the size of a pack of cigarettes and costs around fifty dollars. Every rock and roll musician around the world has one of them in his ditty bag. Fuzz tones are another thing they call them. It is basically over-driving a pre-amp to a point where it distorts.

Years ago the old rock and roll sound used it a lot—that really furry dirty sound. Well, they just turned up the amplifiers until they were about to blow apart. That's o.k. when you're outside, but when you play in a small club you can't turn the amplifiers up to 10—you'll break the front windows. So we get a little device that overdrives the pre-amp at the input stage and you get the same effect as turning up an old tube amplifier and turning it until it begins to smoke.

The new amplifier incorporates many signal processing effects that up to a few years ago were just available as big rake mount jobs and expensive things in the studio.[23]

The electronification of musical instruments is a response to the influence of the recording studios' products and the demand by the audience for a sound equal to what was available on disc or tape.

The existence of a recording permits and is a compelling force for imitation. How many conductors study the score along with a recording? What musician can avoid listening to the ultimate version and not being influenced? When your own act of musicianship is captured and made permanent, it becomes available for self-analysis and criticism. The best record of a particular performance becomes the standard which the performer and competitors must emulate.

The cult of perfectibility has affected and invaded almost all domains of public performance, but the ideal of the *great* performance somehow remains a compelling force for both performer and audience. Admiration of a great performance is still, nevertheless, influenced by our perception of the extraordinary effort together with the risk.

FAKE PERFECTION

In 1977 the dynamic Liza Minnelli danced and sang twelve numbers in a Broadway show. The audience expected and got a high-energy performance from an artist known for her dazzling, exuberant style. That impression is part of that high-risk appeal which lures an audience into the theatre. There was, therefore, a mild uproar when it was disclosed that in three of the twelve numbers Miss Minnelli had been "lip-synching"—appearing to sing, while actually mouthing the words to a pre-recorded tape of herself. Walter Kerr's account of the situation is revealing:

When it was disclosed a few weeks back that Liza Minnelli had managed to save a little of the energy she needs to get through singing and dancing no fewer than 12 numbers . . . by lip-synching three spots in the show, a small flap ensued. It promised to be a rather larger flap than that for the first few minutes—were people who were paying $25 to hear Liza in person really hearing Liza in person or were they under the thumb of a stage manager who was merely pressing buttons on a control panel?—but the instinctive outrage soon subsided. Nerves were soothed by assurances from the Shuberts, who were presenting the standup song parade on Broadway, that no more than two brief moments and one longer spot had been so treated, and then only because no human being could possibly sing and dance so persistently and so feverishly as Liza does and still breathe. We do want our performers to breathe, don't we? And Variety followed up with a substantial editorial defending the practice, mentioning in passing that "Chorus Line" and, very probably, certain other of our folk festivals haven't hesitated to back up their hard-working personnel with mechanical support. If the audience is none the wiser, or doesn't really care all that much, why not?[24]

Walter Kerr goes on to discuss the related issue of using microphones to amplify the actors in an increasing number of theatre productions, but the lip-synching issue touches the core of the problem—that audio electronics are altering a quality valued in performance—risk and effort. The ethical issue is important, but why was Miss Minnelli driven to resort to lip-synching, a common practice in most television shows where recording stars regularly mime their own hit records? Were there no alternatives? Perhaps nine numbers could have been presented instead of twelve. But then the performance would have lost its almost herculean aura; the fact is the audience *expects* Miss Minnelli to breathe while performing twelve difficult energy-draining numbers—for which the audience applauds with abandon. In this case the performer faked the risk and created an atmosphere predicated upon high-risk appeal extraordinary energy. Make no mistake about it, the duplicity was intentional and was based upon the producer's desire to impress the audience with a super-human performance. The defense that very little was lip-synched is irrelevant. The electronically enhanced spots were not identified during the show and therefore the degree of extra-human assistance could not be gauged by the audience. "Perfection" as a value was again confused with "greatness."

THE PERFECT IMPERFECTION

In electronic music, where often the human performer is absent or deemphasized, the matter of the "imperfect" becomes relevant in the impact of a composition.

The Institut de Recherche et Coordination Acoustique/Musique at the Georges Pompidou Center for Contemporary Art in Paris is a laboratory for electronic music research and composition. According to conductor/composer Pierre Boulez, director of IRCAM, "a virtual understanding of contemporary technology ought to form part of the musician's invention."[25] One of IRCAM's stated objectives is "to familiarize both French and foreign composers with the use of computer music techniques and languages which are not yet taught in most music schools."[26] While many of the works composed integrate orchestra, performer, and computer (resulting in some unique performance situations and problems), others are composed using the computer to synthesize and control sound. David Wessel, head of pedagogy at IRCAM, discussed the role of imperfections in the composition process:

> If I were to play for you a performance of a little jazz thing that I have in the computer, I would play it in a perfectly notated fashion. And then I would play it again by simply adding some random mediations to which the notes begin and some random error in the second one more than the first, and, in fact, with the right kind of placement of these imperfections—or random elements—you might say that the second version has much more feeling rhythmically and swings more than the first.
>
> I'm trying to say that with the lack of models of how to really achieve expressive performance, to achieve a sufficient kind of variety in the music, in the face of this lack of deterministic models, or even well-elaborated models which have stochastic elements in them, people revert to rather crude stochastic procedures simply to give some kind of variety or life to the music.
>
> I'm saying that planned imperfections aren't well planned. It is as if you were to add some salt and pepper to food because you didn't have any other kind of taste you wanted. Let's say you're cooking and your spice shelf is rather poor and so you tend to use rather crude means to try to achieve this kind of human expression when faced with the kind of mechanistic perfection that the machine offers.[27]

David Wessel's comments express the extreme reaction to perfect musical expression—that which is too perfect lacks the elements of flaw and error. The truly perfect lacks the substance of human effort. In the case of the absolutely controlled electronic/computerized composition, the response is to improve the perfect by adding a flaw, a perfect mistake—the randomly planned perfect imperfection.

The perfect mistake is the ultimate answer to the search for the

performances which are errorless. But the search is based on the recognition that to err is human and that the inspired performance cannot
be programmed. At the same time, a culture weaned on perfect musical
sound begins to look for that quality in performance. The confusion is
insidious.

THE INSPIRED ERROR

A number of years ago the classical bass virtuoso Gary Karr wrote "The
Ice Age Returneth." It seems appropriate that a musician have the last
word in an essay devoted to the perception of perfection.

> "Perhaps I should not say this, but I am in love with the sound I
> produce on my violin . . . It's so expressive!"—and indeed it was when
> Karlo Mehegan auditioned for the post of violin professor in the de-
> partment of music of the University of Cortesia. The smoke-filled cham-
> ber of cigar-faced pedagogues, all sporting various images of success,
> became lit with bursting unrestrained enthusiasm when the sounds of
> Karlo's violin enveloped the very core of their beings. In their excited
> state of emotional involvement they had forgotten completely the fact
> that the Kreisler *Schone Rosemarin* and the Sarasate *Zigeunerweisen* he was
> playing were not listed in the university's violin curriculum. At the
> conclusion of the presentation, the faculty unconsciously sprang to it's
> feet feverishly applauding, and caressed the artist with exclamations of
> gratitude. The only other candidate for the position was Mayne Turner
> who played Bach's *Chaconne in D Minor* and Beethoven's *Spring Sonata*
> flawlessly, with a dry tone, and greatly impressed the faculty with his
> extraordinary ability to talk and play at the same time—he verbally
> delivered a comprehensive structural analysis of the Beethoven without
> even having missed a single note! This demonstration of artistic flexibil-
> ity could not go unheeded by the professorial ranks and it was this
> special display of academia that won Mayne Turner the position of
> violin instructor at the University of Cortesia (he was awarded an as-
> sociate professorship which paid him an annual salary of $18,000). The
> only lasting memory of Karlo Mehegan's performance was the fact that
> he played two notes out of tune.
>
> Mayne Turner remained in the Cortesia University community until
> his retirement, after having held his appointment for 32 years. His suc-
> cessor was one of his prize pupils who emulated his teacher's analytical
> abilities and intellectual prowess. It is unfortunate however, that this
> young lad was not equipped with Turner's skillful techniques in playing
> the musical game. After five years, he talked himself out of a job. Highly

developed gifts of intellect and analytic procedures gave birth to an unprecedented violin method by which one could translate all musical notation into *words,* thus rendering the violin unnecessary in conveying a musical thought. Cortesia University never again employed a professor of the violin.

Karlo Mehegan was never good with words. His violin said it all! With some Kreisler, Sarasate, Schubert, Bach, or who-have-you, his instrument became a perfect vehicle of expression—it expressed something about Schubert, about Mehegan and about Mehegan's reaction to Schubert. Karlo regarded the notes on paper as documented *musical instructions* which reflect the feelings of the composer. To him, music was a symbol of *emotive life,* and it was with human attitudes that he was most concerned. He perfected his art in order to convey the emotive aspects of the music to use his violin to say what words cannot communicate. He deplored the instrumentalist whose ultimate objective was to achieve technical perfection without any musical or sensuous reason for it. He felt that the musical world was filled with too many mechanics caught up in either the syndrome of the technician or the enveloping web of the academician. All Karlo wanted to do was to play from the heart and he devoted all his concentrated efforts to accomplishing this fulfilling task. He used the academic approach in order to clarify and better understand the composer's documented instructions hoping that it would give insight into the inner emotional attitude of the composer. He advanced his technical flexibility only in order to satisfy and realize both his and the composer's demands.

Karlo Mehegan spent most of his life in search of opportunities to perform, seeking as many outlets as possible in order to share his philosophy of music. Unfortunately, both for Mehegan and the musical public, his violin was heard too infrequently, forcing him to derive his income from selling insurance. About ten years after having struck out at the University of Cortesia, Karlo's undying devotion to the violin finally brought some recognition. This decade of daily toil, interrupted only by the business of insurance, rendered Karlo one of the most consummate artists of the violin the musical world has even known. He was discovered by Impetuous Records who immediately signed him to do two recital albums which they distributed nationally and advertised profusely. The nightmare began in the recording studio with 22 excellent takes; the audio engineers were able to edit and produce a *perfect* musical result which according to Mehegan robbed him of every sense of humanity and turned him into a "cold fish," without the slightest reflection of his emotive life.

According to the contract, the engineers had the final word and before Karlo *knew* it, every record store across the country carried his albums. His only chance for revenge was with his resulting public appearance: he was determined to prove to his already vast listening public that he was not the perfect technical machine created by the taping editors, but a human being overflowing with human feelings who could successfully project these human emotions through the violin. Although Karlo felt that his first concert after the appearance of the record was filled to the brim with feelings, it turned out to be a total flop. The critics lambasted him, declaring in bold type, "Mehegan disappointing compared to his recorded technical perfection." Enraged with this response he continued his course of action with even greater emotive powers, but he was continually met with critical insensitivity. Mehegan's big splash lasted five years until he sank into oblivion. Although the insurance business welcomed the return of Karlo Mehegan, the musical temptations were too great. He is now an assistant professor at the Musquodoboit University, where he teaches music methods and theory.[28]

Six

Talking to Someone Who Isn't There, or Sex and the Single Phone

Without the telephone one would feel disconnected from potential future relationships and from the continuity of present ones. Have you ever met anyone who does not have a telephone? That is highly unlikely, except for those few elite who practice telephone abstinence for short periods or who make a point of dramatizing their anti-social attitudes. When, in 1876, Alexander Graham Bell electronically transmitted the human voice, he changed the lives of every man, woman, and child living in the civilized world. The technology of the telephone has permeated every sector of society, changing traditional interaction among family, colleagues, friends, and daily associates.

A house without a telephone is not a home. An executive is someone who has the telephone answered by someone else. Rules of decorum govern the effective use of the executive phone. Rule number one: never answer your own phone. Rule number two: have your secretary place the caller on hold for a period of time commensurate with that person's status and influence. That maneuver helps the secretaries establish their own status and territory in their strategic manipulation of those calling victims. Family telephone protocol is quickly developed as protection against the invasion of the teenager. Puberty means having your own telephone.

Today, there is nothing mysterious or alien about establishing two-way communication with someone separated from us by distance: there ought to be, but there isn't. Yet, for some the ease of transcending the limitations of space can be disconcerting. A call from London to New York ought to sound as if the involved parties were an Atlantic Ocean apart. One sign of a person's technological age is whether he or she speaks loudly during a long-distance telephone conversation. People over forty tend to raise their voice.

Distance is dissolved in the instant communication between two or more connected parties. Connection is not only accepted, but is *expected*. The exchange of information between Los Angeles and Paris is commonplace, although the means by which that signal reaches its destination is far from ordinary. The fact that people separated by six thousand miles are united by a signal that travels approximately forty-four thousand miles is not important to the conversationalists, but is an extraordinary technological accomplishment facilitated by orbiting satellites.

Immediate auditory connection has become an ordinary event whose mundane nature obscures its social impact. At the same time, the nuances of effect are difficult to precisely describe because the flux of telephonic development is so rapid. The simple telephone connection and its auditory relationships are being altered by the addition of the computer, touchtone dialing, visual display panels, digital transmission, integrated circuits, optical fiber, and bubble storage circuits.

From the user's point of view telephoning is a simple act that requires no particular training beyond learning to dial the correct number and recognizing the meaning of several types of tones or sounds. Our awareness of the technological virtuosity of the telephone has been lost in its constant presence and our dependency on it. No one stops to think about the transformation of the human voice into an electronic signal and its reconversion into recognizable human speech. The technology of the telephone is invisible and subordinate to the interaction of two or more people who communicate with each other though they are separated by space. The essence, the raison d'être, of the telephone was, until recently, human connection (today person/computer and computer/computer connection via a modum is as important as inter-personal communication). The presence of the telephone company as the benign intermediary for the connection has virtually disappeared. The operator, the telephone company's former ambassador of good will, has been replaced by automatic dialing, and the personal encounters which were a part of seeking information, talking to another human being, and arranging a long-distance call have been discouraged by the company because more efficient means have been found. A moment of human contact with an operator can be difficult to find, particularly as recorded voices replace human responses. Perhaps the demonopolized phone companies realized the impact of that non-human mechanical response and an apparent compromise was achieved in which the quest for information begins with operator contact before the customer is transferred to the informative disembodied, slightly metallic, voice of the computer.

For the conversationalists the technology of the telephone is unimportant; the content, the transmission of messages, is paramount. When a call is placed, two options are possible: *to be* connected or *not to be* connected with another person. The ringing of the telephone signals that one party wishes to speak to another. The telephone number is a type of address and it was once assumed that it was fixed. The usual assumption in regard to telephone connections is that two specified locations will be bridged, allowing for communication between two persons. The new telephonic services and technologies provide a number of other options and assumptions.

The President of Bell Laboratories, Ian M. Ross, has stated that the new telecommunications technologies would make it possible "for many people to work, shop, learn, vote, or be entertained from communication consoles located at a point most convenient to them."[1] He described a "mind-boggling spectrum of new services." What are some of the more ordinary new services and conveniences?

Call-screening permits the user to limit incoming calls by controlling the calls that will be accepted. Assuming that individuals know with whom they would normally speak, all other callers could be excluded. "Priority callers could be identified with a distinctive ring, or if the telephone set were equipped with a display, you could see the calling number and then decide whether or not to answer."[2] The unwanted callers could be dealt with in a number of ways. The call would simply not be answered, the excluded would receive a busy signal, or the phone call could be routed to a prerecorded message or could be shunted to an associate prepared to talk to the individual.

If you expect an important telephone call, but cannot get home to receive it, you can call a central office and record a message which will be forwarded to your home. When the call is made to your home your taped voice will be there to answer it and provide the necessary information. Alternatively, the call can simply be forwarded to your current location. Another possibility is a *pocketcoder* that plays back messages received at your home or office from any available telephone without your returning home to receive them.

Instead of each home being assigned a telephone number, each customer can be issued a personal nationwide telephone number. While travelling it is possible to notify the telephone company of each new location by dialing into a network data base and entering a personal code. All calls will be redirected to the new location.

Rudimentary manual tasks such as dialing or redialing can be eliminated: Instead of having to remember constantly used numbers or having to dial long series of digits, numbers can be stored in a phone's memory, and calls can be placed simply by pushing one or two buttons. The automatic callback establishes the connection as soon as a busy telephone becomes free.

Cellular radio is a new form of mobile telephone. While automobile telephones have been around for a long time, cellular radio adds channels and the capacity to serve many more users.

The transformation of the dial into a push-button system has been central to the computerization of the home because the telephone has become the traffic-control center for an unlimited number of services which are now or will shortly be available. Charles L. Brown, chairman of AT&T before that giant company was dismantled, provides this description of future telecommunication services:

> The telephone will become the key to the broad communications and information center—both at home and at the office. People will be able to call up data-storage banks, libraries, newspapers and magazines to request and automatically receive pictures and printed information about news events, fashions, sports, travel books—almost any subject. They may use their phones to vote in elections, to bank by credit, to make and charge purchases from department stores or to play bridge coast-to-coast using video monitors.[3]

MONEY TALKS

One area where touchtone telephone has brought about changes is personal banking, in which numerous types of activities can be handled by telephone: transferring funds from one account to another, stopping payment of checks, and paying bills. Instead of writing out each check, addressing an envelope, affixing a postage stamp, and then delivering the transaction to the mailbox, the telephone circumvents all these tasks. If you have an account with a bank that offers such a service and you provide it with a list of your account numbers with the different merchants or companies that require periodic payment, you can simply call a toll-free number and pay the bills. You have the choice of speaking to one of the bank representatives or using a twelve-button touchtone telephone to "touch-in" instructions to the bank's computer.

> *Computer:* Hello, thank you for calling Bank-by-Phone. Please enter your account number.
>
> (Customer enters in the correct account number using the touchtone buttons.)

The customer never talks to the computer, but the computer does talk to the customer. The human, capable of speech, does not, but the machine, until recently incapable of oral communication, uses the human mode. The interaction continues.

> *Computer:* Please enter your security code.
>
> (Customer enters own code.)
>
> *Computer:* Now please enter merchant number or action code.
>
> (Customer enters the appropriate account number.)
>
> *Computer:* Now please enter amount.

The masculine voice of the computer stresses the polite and civilized transaction.

> (Customer enters the correct sum to be paid.)
>
> *Computer:* Please enter the transaction date.
>
> (Customer follows instructions)

Computer: (recapitulating) Merchant number 1234. Pay the amount of twenty-four dollars and fifty-five cents on August two.

Please enter Merchant number or action code.

The customer continues to enter the rest of the payment requests and upon completion asks for a repetition of all transactions, or requests the total amount paid. The interaction and transactions are officially entered only after the customer pushes the buttons which spell out "BYE." Prior to that point anything or everything can be cancelled. In June 1984 one bank reported that the Bank-by-Phone service continues to grow and that 23.3 percent of the users select the computer mode. Of the telephone customers, 63.8 percent prefer to talk to a bank representative, and some transactions are handled by mail. The figures do not include traditional on-site banking or the use of automatic tellers.

COMPUTER TALK

The speaking computer has a small vocabulary. In this particular case, a human being recorded all of the 255 potential responses that might occur during the interaction. But there are several other ways computers are able to generate speech. A voice response system has been developed which actually creates words rather than selecting them from a lexicon of banking responses. Two hundred words are recorded and broken down into phonics out of which words are then created. It is therefore possible (if all the phonemes are there) to record a voice in one language and produce words in that voice in a second language.

Computers also can synthesize speech. Instead of recording an actual human voice to provide the basic vocabulary from which the computer selects responses, human speech can be simulated using microprocessers. This phase of computer communication is in the developmental stage. At present, the technology requires that human beings communicate with computers nonverbally, but that computers use visual and verbal means. In the future the computer will have the capability of recognizing and understanding the human voice. Albert E. Spencer of Bell Laboratories explains that scientists are working to "enable computers to understand, and hence to respond, to audible human speech. It is important for the man-machine interface of the future that computers be able to hear and understand humans as well as to speak to them. There are only two possibilities . . . either people must learn machine language or vice-versa."[4]

Because the technical nature of transmission is shifting from an analogical signal to a digital one, the type of information processed by a common carrier such as the telephone company has expanded in terms of function and mode. In addition to the transmission of vocal signals, data, facsimile, and video services are available. The future of telephone technology will include important visual components far more sophisticated than the videophone. Ultimately, the marriage of telephone, computer, and television (an electronic ménage à trois) is certain and a variety of interactive functions will be possible.

This partial inventory of future developments indicates changes that will affect everyone in ways for which we are probably not prepared, below the threshold of social awareness, as habits and expectations evolve. The intent of introducing innovative telephone technology is to facilitate communication, not to impede or hinder it. Nevertheless, the acceleration of technological change occurs within a social milieu, and while the telephone answers a very human need for connection, intimacy, security, it also influences that very need. The very concept of the telephone as an instrument aurally connecting two people in different locations is being transformed as telecommunication replaces telephony as the basic metaphor of connection. The image of the old-fashioned operator-run switchboard is still appropriate if the operator is replaced with a computer and the switchboard joins media, data, and people.

"REACH OUT AND TOUCH NO ONE"

In the pre-media era, people must sometimes have longed to talk to another human being over vast distances. It was an impossible dream which became possible. The telephone company's slogan "reach out and touch someone" expresses a basic human desire, although it also suggests some confusion about sensory modality. "Reach out and touch someone"—by making a telephone call—implies that physical presence is achievable through auditory means. It indicates the degree to which the telephone has been integrated into our human interaction. The technology of the telephone vanishes with connection and *only* appears when the coupling is impeded, hindered, or severed. Interference in the circuit, a busy signal, or being cut off because of technical problems indicates the presence of the technology and the institution. It has become natural to communicate with someone else, no matter how far away.

One consequence of telephonic connection is the benign intervention of space between location. Sometimes, telephonically reaching out and touching someone is preferable to physical contact. It is possible to avoid corporal connection and yet communicate. Media connection offers a solution to those who suffer from agoraphobia; perhaps it even redefines that affliction and transforms it into a social grace. It is not necessary to go outside or touch anyone, because it is hardly necessary for communication.

AURAL SEX

Under the "Personals" category, between "Merchandise" and "Pets," of the classified section in *New York Magazine* one can find, each with a number to call:

Lovesaver Hotline—Fantasies explored.
Instant advice. Nothing taboo.

or

Friends' Talkline—Re: fantasies, dreams, and life. No limits.

The cost for the "adult" conversation is $35.00 and can be placed on your VISA or Mastercharge card. The advertisements in the $3.50 type sex magazines are explicit.

Horny?
Phone Sex
Six Calls for the Price of One
Six Calls for $25!
within a 30 day period.
NOW OPEN
We accept Master Card and
Visa or send Money Order to
[name and address excluded][5]

Sex by phone overtly demonstrates "reaching out and touching someone" without the danger or threat of physical intimacy. Psychological aural sex replaces touching the other person.

INTERACTION TO INTERFACE

One indication of how deeply the telephone has become a part of "normal" existence is that some people can disassociate voice and body while talking on the telephone. When you have a telephone conversation with someone whom you have never met, do you supply physical characteristics for that person? Is he or she short, tall, fat, or skinny? How old is the person and what color hair and eyes does the person have? Clearly, it is not important to know the physical characteristics of a person who is giving you flight information over the telephone, but can you listen to a disembodied voice and disregard that the person speaking has a corporeal identity? Some people find it absolutely necessary to imagine a physical and material context for a telephone conversation because they perceive the telephone as merely a means of joining two spaces and thereby allowing for interaction that would normally occur if the two individuals were not separated. The telephone allows people to transcend space which otherwise would impede, certainly discourage, communication, but the telephone relationship is peripheral to *real* relationships. On the other hand, for some people the spatial separation is irrelevant because the relationship has no physical concomitant and only exists because of the presence of the telephone.

But whether the physical context is supplied or not, the communicative act of two persons talking to each other through the medium of the telephone is *true* interaction in which reaction and response flow back and forth dynamically. Communication theorist David D. Berlo states that "in any communication situation, the source and the receiver are interdependent."[6] He defines interdependence as "reciprocal or mutual dependence."[7] Interaction between two or more people is essential to most definitions of human communication. Warren Weaver includes under the rubric of communication "all the procedures by which one mind can affect another."[8] Communication, however, is not restricted or confined to the interaction of individuals who find themselves in a face-to-face situation. Communication between two or more persons is often mediated by a channel which facilitates their interaction even though they might be separated by time and or space. The telephone is one of those media which can facilitate human interactions.

We are prepared for interaction, for the give and take of two-way communication when we answer the ring of the telephone or dial a number, but more and more often we do not reach a human but find ourselves dealing with an intermediary. We then become aware of the interposition of communication technology because we are confronted with it. This confrontation is one for which most people are not really prepared. Solomon J. Buchsbaum, Executive Vice President of Customer Systems at Bell Laboratories dealt with this new relationship when he spoke before the American Society for Information Science.

> Today, in spite of our progress, humans interact with machines in very awkward, stilted ways—via punch cards, keyboards or magnetic tape. The interactions are highly structured. People have to approach machines on the machine's terms, using language and procedures familiar to the machine, not to people.[9]

The means of communicating with machines is changing as computer-synthesized speech and voice recognition is developed. Nevertheless, the relationship with an anthropomorphic machine is quite different from one with a human being . . . or is it possible to confuse one with the other or not care? "The challenge for technologists is to find ways to make these very complex systems easier for average people to use."[10] In the course of a normal day, human beings operate all sorts of complex mechanical marvels. Driving an automobile, operating a dishwasher, or using a gasoline driven lawnmower are simple tasks which must have appeared formidable at first. Do you remember your first encounter with some piece of technology which appeared awesome and perhaps uncontrollable: an electric typewriter, a food processor, a tape recorder, a computer? It is part of growing up in the twentieth century for the technological to become commonplace. This collision of technology and person, the point at which they meet, is referred to by some in technological fields as the "human interface," defined as

> 1. a surface regarded as the common boundary of two bodies of spaces.
> 2. the facts, problems, considerations, theories, practices, etc., shared by two or more disciplines, procedures, or fields of study.[11]

Philip Howard points out that "interface" is one of those words which has been widely adopted as an "imposing metaphor," popularized from the technical jargon of printing, chemistry, and computer technology. "*Interface* is a place where faces meet. It refers to anything that mediates between disparate items: machinery, people, and thought."[12]

> *Interface* is the place at which two independent systems meet and act upon or communicate with each other, as in the *interface* between engineering and science, between man and machine, or more loosely, between the known and the unknown. A secondary and narrower meaning is the method by which interaction or communication is affected between independent systems or disparate items, as in an *interface* between a computer and a typesetting machine.[13]

Human beings interact with each other; perhaps machines interact with each other; but humans "interface" with machines, yet often need not only to interact, but to *communicate*. In this case, it is important to distinguish between *mediated human interaction,* that is communication facilitated by technology, and *mediated interaction with inanimate objects.*

THE UNLOCATION

The usual telephone interaction begins with the initiation of a call by a user who has the telephone number, the correct address, of the individual who is to receive the call. Assume for the moment that the intricacies of connection have been successfully negotiated, that the fingers did not err in haste, and that the intended party has been reached. The conversation is marked by a sense of immediacy and spontaneity: no one can predict for certain what will be said, the reactions, and the outcome. A number of other assumptions are made about the telephone call. An unanswered telephone signals that the person is not at home, because very seldom is anyone able to ignore the enticing ring that could be a mysterious unknown caller, an announcement of an inheritance, or the news of calamity. The ultimate feat of strength and character is *not* answering the telephone: are there people who are so sure of themselves? Not answering the phone is not an act of rejection, of course, unless the calls are being electronically screened (as previously mentioned, now a possibility). Some people abstain, rather than selectively rejecting calls, by disconnecting the phone temporarily in order not to be disturbed.

Once the connection is made, the caller assumes that the person is at the designated telephonic address, and the particular location often influences the substance of the call. The difference in ambience between Grand Central Station and an intimate bedroom *ought* to influence the substance of the call. Generally, each participant imagines a spatial and visual context. The voice issues from a body; there is a visual component to the primarily aural dimension. But there is *nothing* intrinsic in the medium of the telephone that indicates location. Without that information being willingly disclosed or getting clues from background noise, location has to be assumed or asked. (Have you ever asked "where are you?," but doubted the response?)

The concept of location, a definite place, as a component of a telephone call is now no longer certain. The telephone call as a connection of sites, as a bridge between two places where two persons exist, is being replaced conceptually by a connection of people whose space is irrelevant and perhaps private. Because site and telephone number do *not* have to be fixed and since the call can be routed to any place the receiver of the call designates, location is subordinate to the substance of communication. As long as the connection is completed, it does not matter whether a call placed in New York City to a specific location in that city is routed to another part of town or perhaps to Los Angeles. If the purpose of the phone connection is to transfer information, if the emphasis is on data and not on personality, location does not matter or, at least, is secondary. But in some cases not knowing the other person's location during a conversation eliminates a degree of ambience from the interaction the presence of which adds to the tapestry of a relationship.

ANTINOMY OF TELEPHONE SPACE

Ronald Abler states that the "telephone is a *space-adjusting* technique. Telecommunications (like transportation) can change the proximity of places by improving connections between them." [14] We have more relationships and contact with people closer to us and therefore "any technology that makes it easier to contact people at a distance makes it possible to communicate as though that distance had been shortened." [15] However, while the barrier of space has been eliminated, a consciousness of having transcended it is always there. The antinomy of telephone space contrasts the urge to eliminate space with a recognition and *appreciation* that the space exists.

We are thrilled to hear the voice of a loved one who is separated from us by a vast distance and are somewhat frustrated that we are not "there" with the person. "I wish I could just send myself through the wires and be with you" expresses an awareness of space and an appreciation that distance can be attenuated. It is conceivable that the antinomy of distance, in which we are brought close and appreciate distance, is not felt under certain circumstances, but only if the relationship is not personal and/or the call is only to transmit data. Can you imagine receiving a call from a close friend in Europe without being aware of the distance that separates you? The phone is a substitute for a face-to-face encounter and it gets the participants *very* close, *but* without physical presence. Traditionally, the miracle of telephonic communication emphasizes the dimension that has been overcome— *space*.

NO PLACE AMERICA

The "800" telephone number available to companies permits callers from designated geographic areas to place toll-free calls to a specific telephone number for the purpose of requesting service, filing a complaint, or seeking information. Many of the companies have offices all over the United States, but the information or service requested has nothing to do with location and all calls are channeled to a particular telephone office with personnel equipped to serve the customer. A call to such a company representative is purely functional and eliminates a sense of place. And yet the idea of a disembodied voice, lodged from place, is slightly jarring. The "800" exchange conversation takes place in a spatial limbo in which corporate location is irrelevant. The elimination of location changes the social and cultural context of the transaction and emphasizes function and accomplishment. Charm is replaced by efficiency.

THE NON-ANSWERING MACHINE

Communication with a machine is in contradistinction to communication with another human being. The obviousness of that statement should not obscure the far-reaching effects of what appears to be basic, uncomplicated interfacing. We are all subject to subtle changes in our attitudes, values, and customs as new forms of communication are developed and adopted, often involuntarily. For example, no one is immune from the influences of the telephone answering machine.

> "It's time to call my friend to find out whether we are having lunch tomorrow. Here's the number. (How does one describe the process of pushing down the correct buttons, since the dial is passé? Do we still *dial* the number or do we *push* a number?) Ring, ring, ring . . ."
>
> *"Hello, this is your friend. I am not at home right now . . ."*
>
> "Does that mean she does not wish to be disturbed? I bet she's home right now. Damn it! Paranoia again. Why can't I just trust what is being said?"

"No, it's true. I am not home, but I will call you back as soon as I return. Trust me!"

"She says that to everyone I bet. I wonder whether she calls back people she doesn't like."

"At the sound of the beep, you will have thirty seconds to leave a message. Please leave your name . . ."

"She knows my name! She'll recognize my voice . . . She ought to!"

". . . your telephone number and any other intimate things you want to tell me. Thank you."

At this point flop sweat and stage fright begin to develop. Those precious thirty seconds should not be wasted. How to be articulate, suave, and bright? "Where is that beep. 'Beep!!!' That was it!"

"Hi . . . How are you (trying to sound natural, as if I were really talking to her) . . . I was wondering, I mean . . . cancel that!! . . . Can I have another thirty seconds? . . . Are you doing anything tomorrow? . . . (That sounds stupid and sophomoric) I'm not busy. Look . . . I would really like to see you (I am making a fool of myself!) . . . Why don't I call you later? (How many seconds are left?) You know who this is . . . Please call me. Goodbye."

"I didn't even leave my number. I better do the whole thing again . . ."

"Hello, this is your friend. I am not at home right now . . ."

The addition of the answering machine to the accoutrements of communication points to the importance of connection. "Could the telephone have rung while I was out?" Everyone has desperately grappled with the door key attempting to get to the ringing phone *before it is too late*—and failed. Not to miss a connection becomes a compulsion. In some professions disconnection means loss of income, so the anxiety is somewhat understandable. Surprisingly, most physicians do not use such answering units, but hire an answering service which explains that the doctor is not on call and refers another physician if the complaint is serious enough. (Perhaps the medical profession recognizes the latent frustration involved in dealing with an answering machine and assumes they would be dangerous to one's mental health when the body was ailing.) The motivation behind buying an answering machine includes the need to screen calls, a desire to establish status by interposing the machine between oneself and the caller (only busy people require an answering unit), and the neurosis of having to know if someone *might* have tried to call.

The caller's relationship with the answering unit is often strange, sometimes bizarre. Just after the telephone ring is interrupted by the answering voice there is a moment of indecision when the cerebellum has not yet distinguished a recording from the real voice. One breaks off in mid-word with the embarrassing realization that no one is listening. The caller feels a twinge of hostility at being cheated by both the telephone company and by the person being called, the former because it has completed a call to a tape recorder for which there is a charge and the latter because it has reduced a relationship to that of a deposited message.

The public utility does not distinguish between the connection of person to person or person to machine. One is encouraged to dial a number directly, without operator assistance—it is cheaper—but the assumption is that the party being called does not utilize an answering unit or that it is not in operation at that time. It's a new kind of telephonic crap game in which the loser pays for a call without being connected to the person, but to a machine. The game is a bit more exciting and costly with a long-distance call. The solution to the problem would be an answering machine detector which would signal the caller before the connection was made.

Once the tape-recorded instructions begin—"please leave a message after the beep"—anxiety accelerates. The intimidation grows as the time of the magic beep approaches; there is a Pavlovian aspect to the whole affair. Because the device has reduced the caller to a thirty-second response, a surge of adrenalin prepares the victim for a race against the clock. The diabolical machine's egalitarian premise is that anyone can be reduced to thirty seconds. But what happens if only ten seconds of the allotted time are used up? Is that held against the caller? The fact that an innocuous message is being recorded exaggerates its importance. Some people have great difficulty with the knowledge that they are being recorded and quickly hang up without leaving a message (a possibly faltering response suddenly could become a public document). The hang-up percentage must be at least 50 percent. Whether it is intentional or not, the interaction between a caller and the answering machine is manipulative. Instead of a human voice, the caller is greeted by the metallic filtered voice of the respondent politely and cleverly explaining that he or she is not there and that at the sound of the beep one is to leave a coherent message. The focus is shifted from interaction to response, and everyone rehearses for the performance. Not everyone survives the audition and only the select few are "called back." Therefore a great deal of energy is spent in an "answering the tape recorder" game in which a prize is awarded to the clever response. Some people are immune to the contagious game, but a lot of people participate by inventing limericks, obscenities, and bright phrases to captivate and impress the judge. The ultimate test of invention is whether the call is returned and a comment made about one's creative comment. The best of the comments even become part of party talk in which friends are entertained with messages that ill-fated callers left.

Owners of answering machines have to face the reality of phone hang-ups. The number of people who hang up and refuse to perform indicates some antipathy toward this substitute for interpersonal communication. As a result there is maneuvering on both sides of the potential telephone dialogue, the fruition of all this strategy, to persuade the other. The caller seeks to demonstrate a facade that will result in a returned call. The owner of the answering machine seeking to avoid the rejection of the hang-up tries to be equally clever in programming the machine with repartee that will overcome the reluctance some people feel to talk to a machine. One company offers a series of vocal imitations which inform the caller that there's no one available to answer the phone. James Cagney serves as the interlocutor one evening and Jimmy Stewart becomes a subsequent alter-ego. Another company programs the machine with musical jingles.

> PHONE SONGS_{TM} are snappy, up-beat jingles for your telephone answering machine that make it easy and fun to leave (and hear) a message. Makes a great gift. Our jingles are easy to use too. Just play them back on any cassette player into the microphone of your answering machine, just as you would your own voice.
> PHONE SONGS_{TM} come in two formats. Our standard cassette has a selection of five jingles in different musical styles and sells for $15.00. Ask your salesman for a demonstration.
> PHONE SONGS_{TM} is also offering a limited edition of personalized jingles—but only for this Christmas season . . . These jingles offer you (or the giftee) a chance to go into the recording studio and sing on your own jingle over music tracks that have been laid down by professional musicians and jingle singers.[16]

The creators of "Phone Songs," explained that their jingles are intended to "tickle the funny bone, at least to some extent. It warms up the machine experience. It undoes 'mike fright' and predisposes the caller to leave a message."

NONRECIPROCAL IDENTITY

The humor gambit facilitates potential conversation and therefore its motivation is quite understandable. There are several examples of the telephone functioning *not* to facilitate dialogue between human beings, but rather to serve them. The "Dial-it" services exist for very specific uni-directional communication purposes. Dial-a-Joke, Horoscopes-by-Phone, National Sports, the weather, time, Dow Jones, Dial Dr. Joyce Brothers *et al.* offer no expectations of interaction, merely satisfaction of a specific need.

On the other hand, there are situations in which the caller needs to interact with a computer via the central medium of the telephone. The concept of telephone dialogue with a computer, and it must be stressed at this point that only the phenomenon of aural/oral telephonic interaction with a computer is being discussed, is at first staggering for someone who believed that if your pet rock answered, you were in deep trouble. One of the problems inherent in the dialogue (if it can be called that) with such a computer is that it does not involve equals. While all human beings are theoretically born equal, computers and human beings are not, although dialogue between them suggests some degree of parity. An object that talks is more human that one that does not talk. The problem with the dialogue is that one confuses "interface" with "interaction," that the expectations of human communication become confused with those of the machine.

Even more important than location in most communication relationships is identity. Most people want and need to know with whom they are talking during a non-face-to-face interaction. Yet, at times, it takes several seconds to determine whether the voice on the other end of the line is a live human voice, a computer-controlled tape of human speech, or a computer's simulation of human speech. The communicative exchange seems incomplete as long as one of the parties remains anonymous—either in name or personality.

Most of us have been called by a company which either got our name from an available list or randomly selected the number. The caller might volunteer his or her own name and that of the organization, then proceed to read a series of prepared enticements all aimed at getting us to buy, donate, or subscribe, but at no time does the caller reveal anything personal about himself or herself. It is as if we were conversing or rather listening to a facsimile of a human being. The ultimate act of dehumanization is the machine-like caller who immediately addresses us by first name in an emotionless voice which reeks of boredom and efficiency. "Gary, I'm Fred and I'm calling on behalf of the Charitable Organizations of the Galaxy and we would like some of your time and *money . . ."*

The reciprocity of identity is essential to dialogue. But a computer has neither a location or identity. Whom are we talking to when we talk to a computer? Institutional identity, Mr. and Mrs. Bank, might be charming, but it remains an artificial facade. The fact is that at the other end is a computer synthesizing speech—a piece of machinery full of mysterious transistors, chips, and circuits, that has been created by engineers to serve humans. But that is difficult to keep in mind during the dialogue, for the tendency to anthropomorphize the computer is strong. This impulse is common in relationships with all sorts of inanimate objects, from ships and planes to automobiles and camera. Why is an airplane feminine? Why do some people name their homes? It is difficult enough not to ascribe or attribute human characteristics to a "silent" computer, but when it can talk, the tendency is difficult, if not impossible, to avoid. Is it possible to ever talk to a machine without giving it some sense of our *own* humanness?

Companies involved in the development of talking computers have recognized the difficulty that people have conversing with machines and have found that in some situations employees require the computer's voice to be personalized. One large oil company installed a computer system to handle credit card authorizations from gas stations all over the country. The people who use the system are often part-time service station attendants with little job motivation and not much longevity. Since attendants found it very difficult to pick up a phone and interact with a functional computer's voice, management decided to give the system a personality. "We gave it a name, a physical personality. The system is called Marcy."[17] Marcy was also the person who appeared in the brochures, sales training material, and videotapes that were distributed. The same actress whose voice was recorded to serve as the computer's voice became the sales personality.

In the past, the telephone was an instrument which eliminated distance by transcending space. The miracle of that feat has vanished with the public's dependence on immediate oral/aural connection without conciousness of distance. With instant connection a distinct possibility, the need to control the instrument was introduced. To some extent, the caller and the called have been transformed into adversaries. Incoming calls are controlled through secretaries, answering services, answering units, and screening devices. Both caller and called now can exist in non-space, that is the telephone address and an actual address do not have to physically correspond. Location can be disguised, and in the case of the special 800 number is irrelevant. The addition of computer-controlled vocal responses further destroys the clarity of connection. Not only is it not always possible to know where the called party is once called, but it is also not immediately clear whether the voice is a human one. It is somewhat alarming to think of an individual seeking and receiving sexual gratification over the telephone, but think for a moment . . . maybe that wasn't a person.

Seven

The Last Person Who Knew Everything

In that Neanderthal age before the television era, I would cease any and all activities in order to enter the fantasy world of radio each weekday between 4:00 and 6:00 p.m. It was radio serial time.

> Look! Up in the sky! It's a bird! It's a plane! It's Superman! More powerful than a locomotive! Faster than a speeding bullet! Superman! Visitor from a strange planet, with powers and abilities far beyond those of mortal man!

For a short time I escaped into the world of a dynamic figure whose strength, ability, and power were unsurpassed on Earth. This was a figure who could be counted on, who, in addition to being powerful, must surely have known all there was to know (it would never have occurred to anyone that Superman could be a dummy). This was not the Superman of the 1980 film fame, whose stupidity almost reduced him to human dimensions, but a hero who transcended all human flaws and frailties, who could save us all during a time of chaos and emergency. We believed!

But times have changed. In 1980 the prologue to a special promotional issue of a Superman comic book prepared for the Radio Shack Company teased the reader with the following:

> A cry for help . . . a rush of wind . . . and the world' s greatest Superhero hurtles into action once more . . . while, miles below, in Metropolis, two young heroes sit at their TRS-80 computers, their fingers flying urgently across the keyboards. What is the astonishing connection between these two events? Read on . . . and see.

"The Computers that Saved Metropolis" finds Superman incapacitated by millions of microscopic Kryptonite crystals that an extraterrestial anti-hero has released into the air. When they attack Superman's nerve cells he is reduced to a mere powerful force unable to think, incapable of protecting the people of Metropolis from the destruction that is about to be unleashed upon them by the dastardly "Major Disaster."

And who are the human heros with nimble fingers who will soon come to the aid of Superman? They are high school students whose comic book dialogue indicates something other than enchantment with education.

> YAWNNN. Just what we've been waiting for, Ms. Wilson . . . A boring talk on computers. I can't think of anything I'd rather hear about . . . except maybe the history of brussel sprouts.

When Superman visits the classroom to lecture on computers, not knowing that fate would soon place the destiny of millions of people in the hands of two members of the audience, the students response is less than enthusiastic. "Someone wake me up when he's finished! History and computers are boring enough by themselves, but together? Good night!" Of course, since Superman still possesses all of his admired faculties, he uses his charm and persuasive powers to win over the recalcitrant monsters.

The crisis created by Major Disaster is awesome as all of the major computers in Metropolis fail—as well as Superman's computer-like brain. Superman explains:

> My super-brain, Alec, controls my powers in much the same way those big companies perform their functions. Major Disaster was smart enough to know I could have rigged up a micro-wave relay with one of those computer systems.

Shanna, one of the potential delinquents who will come to the aid of the superhero immediately comprehends: "The computers could do the

Computer literacy comes to the aid of a weakened Superman incapable of saving Metropolis from that archfiend Major Disaster. Moral I: even juvenile delinquents have a place in the world—if they learn to operate a computer. Moral II: Superman is no longer omnipotent. Moral III: nimble fingers are valued as much as a wise mind.

instant computations and calculations your brain would normally do, so you could still use your super-powers."

> Right on the button, Shanna! Major Disaster was thorough enough to knock every "major" computer out of commission . . . but two certain micro-computers he couldn't possibly have known about . . . your TRS-80's . . . and two volunteers! Who . . .?

As a jetliner hit by lightning plunges to the ground, Superman, hooked up by microphone to the incomparable illiterate duo, calls for help!

> All right, team, here goes! According to my super-vision: jetliner is plummeting on a 44 degree downward course at 505 miles per hour . . . and gravity is pulling downward at 32 feet per second! In addition—the thunderstorm is whipping up a power wind toward me at 63 miles per hour! I should compensate for the wind and still reach the jetliner before it crashes to the ground.

The nature of Superman's intellectual capacities is puzzling. Clearly, anyone who can calculate the speed of the downward course of a plane ought to be able to follow through without the help of microcomputers or of two potential delinquents. It does all work out in the end as once again Superman comes to the rescue—with the aid of Shanna, Alec, and the TRS-80 microcomputers. The world is changing along with the fantasies of yesterday.

Walter Ong has stated "if knowledge is power, knowledge of how to generate knowledge is power over power.[1] In the case of "The Computers that Saved Metropolis" the fate of an entire population is placed in the hands of two young people whose strength is their digital dexterity rather than acquired knowledge or wisdom. The shift in the image of power—from the fantasy of the incomparable Superman to a pair of vulnerable semi-literate teenagers—is a startling demonstration of a shift in values. Only the naive and the young believe and identify with a superman-like hero, probably because there is a need for such a symbolic figure at that stage of life and during that cultural period. But fantasy exists within the framework of reality and Superman born in the turbulent late 1930's is somehow reduced to absurdity when placed in the fictional milieu of the 1980's, where the fantasies of yesterday have become part of today's commonplace reality. My relationship to Superman has been changed forever, not only because I have been forced to grow up, but also because he has been revealed as vulnerable and his power has been proven to be finite. And he has been helped not by the gentle child, but by the ignorant one who has access to the holy font.

THE LIBRARY

One example of the changing attitude toward knowledge is the recent dedication of a new Educational Resource Center at Clarkson College, a multimillion "library of the future," which includes the latest learning technology: computers, videotape decks, slide projectors, and a television studio. The President of Clarkson College asserted that "books can be too slow."

> Clarkson, which specializes in science, technology, and management, has more books today in its new information center, than it had in the library it abolished, Dr. Plane says—140,000 volumes against 130,000. But for information needed fast and not to be "retained for a long period," the computer system is preferred, he adds.
>
> "It's been a real hit with the students," he notes. "You almost have to stand in line. Every seat is taken."
>
> With a satellite hook-up, the student body of 3,500 has access to data bases in the nation that list all the books by an author, often provides an abstract of each work and tell where to get the books, Dr. Plane observes.
>
> A serendipitous benefit, the college chief says, is that freshman are developing "new skills in spelling and typing—because that's the only way you can communicate with a computer."[2]

Russell Baker's reactions to this innovative library of the future was less than gracious, although acerbically perceptive. While accepting the notion that students will graduate from the university "stuffed" full of information, he nevertheless asks, "What does this have to do with education?"[3] In response to the director of the Educational Resource Center who asserts that "education . . . is basically an information transfer process," Mr. Bakers replies:

> "Information-transfer process" indeed. Education is not like a decal, to be slopped off a piece of still paper and pasted on the back of the skull. The point of education is to waken innocent minds to a suspicion of information.
>
> If you're going to learn the importance of mistrusting information, somebody first has to give you some information, and college is a place where people try to do this, if only so that professors can find out how gullible you are.

Knowing that, they can then begin to try to teach you to ask a few questions before buying the Brooklyn Bridge or the newest theory about the wherefore of the universe. I'm talking about the good professors now, not the ones who spend all their time compiling fresh information to be transferred to the book-buying public. Even the good professors, however, rarely have enough time to teach the whole student body the art of doubting, which leads to the astonishing act of thinking.[4]

Mistrusting information requires a higher order of cognition than acquiring facts, but today we place a greater priority upon functional information than upon the serendipitous exploration of a body of knowledge. A technological world requires specialized skills to operate and service the institutions which are its constitutents. Therefore, the relationship between scholar and technologist has changed. The scholar becomes obsolete as the need for superskills outweighs that for superminds.

THE REPOSITORY OF KNOWLEDGE

The thirty volumes of *The Encyclopedia Britannica* include a total of 43 million words. These thirty volumes require one tenth of a cubic inch of computer memory—the size of a match head—for storage. Assuming the availability of this information through a computer which allows for storage and retrieval, who would oppose a more efficient means of preserving information than in those heavy bulky volumes? Instead of one impressive dust-catching bookshelf, a visual display screen is substituted on which the desired or required information unrolls. The shift from the book as storage device to computer is clear and irreversible.

Each new repository of knowledge has a monumental effect upon subsequent ages. The revolutionary effects of a medium upon knowledge have been the subject of numerous writers. Eric A. Havelock's *Preface to Plato* is a fascinating analysis of the Greek cultural tradition and an account of Plato's opposition to poetry. Havelock states, "All human civilizations rely on a sort of cultural 'book,' that is, on the capacity to put information in storage in order to reuse it."[5] In that sense, Havelock's analysis of an Homeric epic as an oral encyclopedia of knowledge sharply contrasts with the image of computer memory the size of a match head. A number of questions arise. How many match heads will be required to store the entire record of human civilization? Will past cultures be indexed on the basis of how much computer memory is required for their storage?

Harold Innis, the intellectual parent of Marshall McLuhan, maintains that every medium of communication has an inherent bias toward time and space, a bias which shapes the nature of each culture. In *The Bias of Communication* Innis says:

> A medium of communication has an important influence on the dissemination of knowledge over space and over time and it becomes necessary to study its cultural setting. According to its characteristics it may be better suited to the dissemination of knowledge over time than over space, particularly if the medium is heavy and durable and not suited to transportation, or to the dissemination of knowledge over space than over time, particularly if the medium is light and easily transported. The relative emphasis on time or space will imply a bias of significance to the culture in which it is imbedded.[6]

In his analysis of the acceleration of knowledge in relationship to the development of media, Walter Ong observes that knowledge became increasingly stored outside the human mind through writing, print, and ultimately electronic media. But cultures influenced "by the changes induced by new knowledge storage and retrieval and communication developments are never entirely aware of what changes are. Hence of necessity they lean on obsolescence and even find obsolescence exciting."[7] Ong's judgment about the impact of the coalescence of a storage medium and knowledge is noteworthy.

> For the advancement of learning, storage of knowledge is essential, but insofar as knowledge is mere "information" or "structure" its storage and retrieval are not truly intellectual tasks. As artificial extramental information storage and retrieval systems (writing, print, and electronics) evolved, the mind was freed more and more to do its proper work of thinking, and the acceleration of knowledge got under way.[8]

The growth of knowledge has accelerated during the past decade, and the momentum can be linked to the phenomenal growth of computer technology and its absorption into the general activities of contemporary existence. Has the pace of the computer's penetration into daily life been uniform in all disciplines? My intuition is that the growth has been unequal. It can be safely assumed that the sciences have far outstripped the humanities in their discovery and growth. The quantifiable nature of science lends itself to storage and retrieval. The growth of technology is geometric, while our ability to deal with that technology is arithmetic. As a result, the specialist, someone who accumulates all the information and skills in a particular subject, develops.

The generalist is the contemporary dinosaur of knowledge, much to be admired, but not very helpful in the process of practical living. The age of specialization has clearly arrived in the business and scientific worlds. Lawyers practice corporate law, criminal law, communication law, estate planning, marital and family law, insurance law, property law, ad nauseam. Physicians are experts in allergies and immunology, cardiology, psychiatry, colon and rectal surgery, dermatology, endocrinology and metabolism, gastroenterology, geriatrics, hematology, internal medicine, oncology, nephrology, neurology, ad nauseam. Even in the elevated halls of humanistic academia the dissertation focuses on the literature of the Cromwellian age; the linguist learns all there is to be known about the Marathi language of India; and the musicologist studies the derivation and use of the *Dies irae* by contemporary composers. Somehow the less practical specialist is still to be admired—perhaps because the discipline or body of knowledge is not critical for the world to continue.

THE KRYPTON FACTOR

One wonders whether our basic attitudes toward the acquisition of knowledge are changing. Is knowledge for its own sake still to be considered admirable, an ideal? What would the generalist be able to contribute if, as in Mark Twain's *A Connecticut Yankee in King Arthur's Court,* he or she were suddenly transported to medieval England equipped with the sophisticated awareness of the 1980's? What is it we could invent? A match, a motor, a gun, a doorbell?

Several years ago the American Broadcasting Company ran a summer program entitled *The Krypton Factor.*

> In every civilization man has searched for the ultimate combination of intelligence and physical ability in one super being. Tonight you'll witness this unique search. This is the challenge of "The Krypton Factor."

My interest in the search for the "ultimate" strong-wise person assured my rapt attention—the ideal combination: wisdom and physicality. What is the "Krypton Factor?" What is krypton? Did it not have something to do with Superman? Isn't it merely a type of gas? Indeed, it is a rare inert gaseous element discovered by Sir W. Ramsay, but as any true scholar knows, the name comes from the Greek "krupton, neut. of kruptos" meaning hidden or secret, from which we get the word crypt.

So it is a hidden ingredient which provides insight, wisdom, and strength. The host, Dick Clark of *American Bandstand,* welcomes the national audience and introduces the program.

> Tonight, we're going to experience the challenge of the Krypton Factor—the ultimate test of mental and physical abilities. You're going to get to know these four exceptional people who will be challenged to their very limits. The challenger who achieves the highest Krypton Factor moves on to the Krypton finals and has the opportunity to win a total of fifty thousand dollars in gold.
>
> The challenge of the Krypton Factor begins now. It's phase one. Your first challenge tonight is an electronic car chase called "Dodg'em." This will be a test of hand-eye coordination in reflex speed. Take a look at the big screen. You'll see two cars and a maze of roads. The electronic computer controls the car on the left. You control the car on the right using the lever on your podium. You'll play one at a time against the computer. Your job is to avoid a head-on collision for ten seconds. If you're successful, you'll receive five points.

The excitement and tension mounts as each of the four contestants faces the unpredictability of a computer programmed to outwit its human opponent. It is a one-on-one competition: person against machine.

Phase two is a bit different: a test of mental agility.

> It's tough. It demands your fullest concentration . . . There are two levels of this phase, for the maximum total of ten points. If you miss you will be eliminated from this phase. Test number one is called "return trip." This is where you must reverse a trip through various cities. You must repeat them back in reverse order. For instance, if I say Seattle, Portland, Sacramento, you must put them in reverse order and give me Sacramento, Portland, Seattle. Except that there will be five cities. You'll have ten seconds in which to answer.
>
> The second level in phase two is a numbers game. This is where you will be given a six-step mathematical problem using addition, subtraction, multiplication, and division. There will be six numbers and you will have ten seconds in which to answer . . . Stand by Susan! Here is your test! 3 times 7 plus 3 divided by 6 times 1 minus 4.

Susan gives the correct answer and the rest of the contestants follow in their attempt to solve these intricate problems. Phase three begins after a commercial for Kentucky Fried Chicken and Five Alive Fruit drinks (the subtle associations cannot be avoided: chicken plus fruit drink equals wisdom and strength).

Phase three, which has been videotaped earlier on location, tests physical ability. The Krypton Challenge Course

> was especially designed to be fair to all competitors, male or female. No one has a clear cut advantage. It all starts here at the "slide for life." A quick run takes the challengers to the balance beams. These are a little tricky. On the other side our competitors crawl through these twisting tubes. Then they must run to the high-powered jet skis and race them across the lake to the shore. We will watch the action from up in the sky from our helicopter camera. And they have to leave the boats. Off to the swings. At the swings they must swing until they kick their color button which releases the door. Then they run to the awaiting moon walkers in the home stretch to the finish line . . .

Phase four is the "observation phase" in which the contestants watch two short excerpts from the movie "The Legend of the Lone Ranger." "How many rifles were mounted on the wall? Six or seven?" "What car came between the coal tender and the club car?" "Did the gang leader move the train [a model] with his left or right hand?" Then all the contestants are asked, "which of the six actors in front of you played the role of the man who tied Tonto's hands as he stood on the gallows." No one guessed correctly. Time for another commercial after all of this excitement—Burger King and Black Flag Exterminator (the associations don't seem to apply, do they?).

The final portion of the program is the "catchup phase." The key is instinct, knowledge, and speed. The first person to lock in (push the button) has the chance to answer the question and either win two points for the correct answer, or lose two points. Halfway through this phase the value of the questions is doubled. The questions are asked at breakneck speed, and some are not even completed as the contestants interrupt with their answers.

> What Florida State football player has become one of the biggest box office movie stars in the world?
>
> The pommel horse event is in which Olympic sport?
>
> The "goober" is another word for . . . ?
>
> In the Peanut's comic strip, what is the name of Snoopy's bird friend?
>
> A good stock of matzoh ball soup is made from stewing what kind . . . ?
>
> Amman is the capital of what . . . ?

Who is the chief editor and founder of the *National Review* magazine?

A bucking bull was featured in what John Travolta . . . ?

Walden Pond was the home . . .

Is this the "ultimate test of mental and physical ability"? What a fascinating and depressing display of mediocrity! It is fair and necessary to condemn such a show because of its infantile approach and moronic level of appeal. It would be unfair to generalize about the intellectual state of the world on the basis of one such show. But the program did cause me to reflect on our attitudes toward knowledge. Is *The Krypton Factor* symptomatic of a shift? What is measured in the program is quickness, agility, and image retention, but definitely no form of ratiocination. Perhaps the rapid pace of contemporary television does not allow for anything but the quick stroke, the non-thought.

THE KNOWLEDGE GAME

My preoccupation with quiz shows is similar to the "Secret Life of Walter Mitty" syndrome as I assume the identity of the challenger hoping to dazzle the world with an unlimited store of knowledge. The desire to acquire or devour knowledge, to know more than anyone else in the world, is an unrealistic and impossible ambition, but it was also a secret, burning wish of a childlike being gifted with an insatiable desire to know. What foolishness! But what a thought-provoking idea— to know everything there is to be known. Was there ever a time when the world was so simple that it would have been possible? Who was the last person who thought it possible and attempted the arduous task? Could it have been Denis Diderot, the eighteenth century French Encyclopedist, or René Descartes, the seventeenth century French philosopher and mathematician? Could it have been the great Aristotle or Rome's Cicero?

The knowledge game exhilarates and frustrates as the player struggles toward an elusive goal that is always receding. In *Man's Unconquerable Mind*, Gilbert Highet describes the compelling force that attracts the intellectual Don Quixote.

The Book of Job puts into poetry one of the central experiences of every human being. It is an experience which begins early in childhood, which (unless it is benumbed or smothered) lasts into extreme old age, which often drives men further than other passions, and which has produced far more of the achievements that distinguish us from the beasts. It is a sense of wonder.[9]

It is this sense of wonder which "combines the wish to know with the knowledge that all cannot be known."[10] The romance of Highet's "astonished awareness of inflowing mystery"[11] is offset by the practical necessities of functioning, surviving, living from day to day. Bertrand Russell has said, "What passes for knowledge is of two kinds: first, knowledge of facts, second, knowledge of the general connection between facts."[12] It is necessary to distinguish between facts and connections, to distinguish between knowledge and information, because the relationships are being radically altered as the computer begins to transform this technological age. At this point it might be helpful to provide a simple definition of "information." The *Random House Dictionary*'s first definition is "knowledge communicated or received concerning a particular fact or circumstance."[13] A number of other definitions are supplied, but of particular interest is the discussion of synonyms of "information."

> INFORMATION, KNOWLEDGE, WISDOM are terms for human acquirements through reading, study, and practical experience. INFORMATION apples to facts told, read, or communicated which may be unorganized and even unrelated: *to pick up useful information.* KNOWLEDGE is an organized body of facts: *a knowledge of chemistry.* WISDOM is a knowledge of people, life and conduct, with the facts so thoroughly assimilated as to have produced sagacity, judgment, and insight: *to use wisdom in handling people.*[14]

The distinguishing factors of information are connection, organization and application—all of which are judged by the criterion of utility.

THE NEW UTILITY

The computer is developing into a multi-functional utility serving the needs of industry, education, business, medicine, entertainment, and the home.

> The new IT [information technology] represents the convergence of computer, or rather information processing technologies and telecommunication technologies on the basis of an "enabling" micro-electronic infrastructure.[15]

In March of 1981 an elaborate brochure announced that the First Information Utilities Conference would be held in New York.

> In basic terms, information utilities can be defined as those systems, services and pieces of equipment that bring varied types of information into the office and the home.
>
> Information Utilities are products and services that deliver information: (1) to large volumes of users (2) at prices low enough so that each transaction is made routinely, not as a separate purchasing decision.[16]

At times the language of the publicity becomes somewhat bombastic.

> Why an information utilities conference now? The time is ripe. New technologies, new-data bases, new tests, new pilot projects are coming at a furious rate . . . And the prize is the richest of all; the North American continent. Not fragmented like Europe, not hung up on nationally-sponsored technologies . . . but a true brawling frontier of competing forces wresting for billion dollar payoffs.[17]

Information Utility services are based upon the possibility of two-way communication and the interfacing of display screen, telephone, response unit, and computer. The potential of the system and its components is staggering as it provides each user computational and informational capabilities whenever desired. The screen serves a variety of functions, including the display of alpha-numeric information and slow scan or regular television signals. The information utility service is now available to the public and a counterpart non-public service has been indispensable to government, education, business, medicine, and research for some time now. It would be difficult to come up with a definitive, complete IT inventory, because there are so many variations and so many daily developments. Among the services are teletext and view data, electronic yellow pages, computer graphics, electronic mail, teleshopping, video-conferencing, electronic banking, voting, testing, monitoring, surveillance—the list continues.

This extraordinary cornucopia of data rests upon a structure of people, services, and organizations which gather and update the special collections of facts, figures, and abstracts which are the "databases" available to the alpha-numeric consumer. A combination of assemblers and vendors provide an incredible variety of databanks. The SOURCE, describing itself as America's Information Utility, offers a news retrieval service, an electronic mail system, free classified ad bulletin boards, stockmarket data, an electronic travel service, airline schedules, a restaurant and hotel guide, electronic games and a number of other conveniences.

It is in the very nature of computer technology and services that the stress is on *useful* information as it is stored, retrieved, processed and fed back to the consumer's various needs. Discrete items are stored in the memories of computers and are available upon demand by themselves or in conjunction with other data that has been similarly processed. But whether the data is used to establish long-term economic trends, as a primary research resource in a specific academic discipline, or to correlate separate trends in order to project future needs, the emphasis is on providing subscribers with *information* that can be *useful.* According to IBM, "if you can't retrieve it, it's *useless* to us." The stress is on the quick and efficient response to almost any query. Whether the subscriber is a large corporation with its own on-line terminal or a home user connected through a microcomputer or an interactive cable system, useful information for a specific need is requested. The leisurely pursuit of knowledge is antithetical to the computer game. Indeed, leisure and the data bank are incompatible as the customer pays for time and efficiency. While general perusal is possible it is an unlikely prospect, discouraged by the functional nature of purchasing time and product. The computer as a medium of communication and information transforms knowledge into a viable commodity which can be collected, stored, retrieved and utilized for a specific purpose.

THE ELECTRONIC LIBRARY

Is a computer retrieval system so radically different from the traditional library? The library *is* a retrieval system and the book is a form of storage, although our expectations of a library are different from what we expect of a computerized information system. The old library search for a book included two tasks: finding the subject, author, title, and call letter in the card catalogue, and actually acquiring the book itself. In early 1985 the main branch of the New York Public Library eliminated the card catalogue system and replaced it with computer terminals. Looking for a book places the responsibility for the search upon the person who seeks the volume, while the electronic catalogue search shifts the focus to the swift, almost magical machinations of the computer. The expectation is for a quick result. There isn't anything particularly wonderful to be celebrated in the long laborious library search.

Efficiency is to be preferred to inefficiency, but at the same time, the quality of physically acquiring the work is different when one contrasts the electronic reception of material with the task of actually meandering down library aisles seeking the precious sought-for book. The ambience and the serendipity of coming upon things of interest incidental to the goal of the search are lost. The possibility of an accidental brush with a captivating tome always hovers over the narrow passages of the library stacks.

The comparison of the printed page of a book and an alphanumeric page on a display screen is not one of print versus non-print since both forms are read, although the sense of tactility is clearly absent from the display screen. The smell and touch of ink, paper, and binding are replaced by the mesmerizing brilliant glow of symbols and the star-like quality of the characters as they flash on the screen.

The book can be compared with its computer equivalent on the bases of context and selection. The confrontation of reader and display screen occurs in a somewhat restrictive setting. A particular physical environment is required in which one sits attentively looking directly at a display screen. An oblique glance is impossible. The book does not have to be plugged into an electrical outlet to assume existence. Its portable non-contextually restrictive life allows it to be read almost anywhere, in almost any posture—as long as the eyes meet the surface of the page—and at random, unplanned moments during the day.

Selection is a different matter. Whereas it is easy for a subscriber to almost instantly retrieve pages of different documents or books through a computer system, a decision must be made to request a specific discrete item; to retain the image on the screen, whether to go on to the next page (the material displayed on the screen at any one time is considered equivalent to a page), or whether to record the page on a disc or print it out onto paper. It is conceivable that an electronic system might be used to read a novel or for the pleasurable, non-economically productive perusal of non-fiction material, although my old-fashioned romantic notion of reading dismisses that notion; one does not cuddle up with a computer by a pleasant warm fire or take it to bed for a good read shortly before going to sleep.

The electronic page is a nonphysical entity sandwiched between the nonexistent covers of the computer book. It has no physical context as it is isolated from its binary resting place and unrolls upon the screen. The page of the traditional (old-fashioned?) book is read, but never

isolated from the adjacent pages. Turning the page with the long acquired skill of the nimble movement of the index finger (either with
the left or right hand) is comparable, in function, to pushing the proper
keyboard symbol, but it is an act of a different medium in which a
new tactile sense affects the reader's psychological sense of the material
apprehended. The distinction between readers' attitudes to books and
display screens has its roots in the presence or absence of a physical
object which can be identified as the physical manifestation of the work.
Perhaps the floppy disc is the counterpart of the book, although it can
never be read without the electro-mechanical device which scans the
magnetic surfaces.

In many cases the "book as object" has no equivalency in the world
of computerized information, since the interfacing of computers, data
bases, data banks draws material from a variety of sources. The requested information can come from several data bases and be assembled
for the moment on that particular terminal and screen.

The intent here is not to sing the praises of the book over the
computer, but rather to indicate that in a period when an increasing
amount of information is being transported to homes and offices via
interactive media systems, our attitudes toward knowledge and information begin to change because of (1) the sheer amount of data available and (2) the nature of the medium used to transmit it.

THE INFORMATION EXPLOSION

The scope and magnitude of the "fallout" from the world wide "information explosion" is hardly understood. On the international level, nations are debating the implications of the "free flow of information."
International bodies such as UNESCO have been deliberating over the
development of a "New World Information Order" as emerging nations demand greater control over their media and information desti-
nies and accuse the developed nations of media imperialism. Important
questions are being asked. Is the high-speed transmission of data over
the airspace of nations a violation of national sovereignty? Can the
people of a nation be violated by information and ideas not relevant to
the current issues and problems their country faces? In *The Geopolitics
of Information: How Western Culture Dominates the World,* Anthony Smith
describes the "New International Electronic Order" and indicates how
new developments in electronics have expanded the concept of "infor-

mation" during the past two decades.[18] Smith outlines the connection between information and commodity. "In the era of the computer, information has come to be seen as the raw material which, when reduced to the dot-and-dash binary codes which computers use, can be bought and sold as a commodity itself."[19]

There is suddenly concern over too little and too much information, data pollution, and privacy when interconnection is needed and vital to daily transactions. There cannot be any doubt that the information utility will develop into an important force throughout the world and that as we reap the harvest of benefits, a host of knotty problems will also be introduced. There can be no doubt that individuals living in the telecommunications world of the 1980s *must* interact and conduct relationships with a variety of institutions in which communication is facilitated by a computer. Who has not experienced the frustration of trying to convince some well-meaning employee, who goes by the rules, that an error has been made, that the computer is wrong?

The Incredible "Fact" Machine

Fantasize for a moment that an amazing fact machine exists, which instantly provides the correct answer to any question that can be responded to with a statement of fact, and is so small it can be carried everywhere. What would you expect the owner of this machine to "know" *that could not be recovered or retrieved through this magical machine?* What would it be necessary to know in order to exist from day to day if one could be plugged into this incredible fact machine?

What are your expectations of someone merely equipped with the more conventional unassisted, but educated brain? What should the moderately literate person know not merely to subsist, but to thrive? The question is somewhat naive, but most of us have thought and measured ourselves in terms of what we know or should know. The richness of personality includes both a personal history of accomplishment and a storehouse of accumulated trivia, awareness, and general information that we call knowledge. It is assumed that an educated person has accumulated more knowledge than a less educated individual. To some extent, we all judge each other by the capacity of the human brain to amass and store a reservoir of experience and data which exceeds that which is required for self-preservation: a nonpurposive accumulation of information. There are certain things that must be known if one is to become an accountant, a dentist, a teacher of English. But are there things that need not be known if it is understood where to find that which is needed? Is it adequate to know where to find required information? Is there any particular vital reason why one should know that Columbus discovered the New World in 1492 or that Gutenberg invented movable type in the middle of the fifteenth century? Is there a valid reason why students should be subjected to the tyranny of testing and be forced to remember the date for the Magna Carta or the combatants in the War of Roses when that information is readily available whenever it is desired? Is not the computer transplant a suitable connection to instant information? The pedagogue's response is that learning is "good for the student," that the means and discipline of acquiring knowledge somehow add character and depth that make an individual interesting and vital. The rationale for the time-honored tradition of learning is undermined by the presence of the magical fact machine which blesses forgetting, because nothing is irretrievable.

Ye Olde Memory

There was a time when memory was the chief means of transmitting a social heritage from one generation to the next. The development, however, of extramental means of storage deemphasized the need to learn by rote. Hence, the further sophistication of storage and retrieval devices shifted more and more of the burden of memorization from the brain to an electronic device—in this case, the computer. The de-memorization of knowledge is accompanied by an increase in the specificity and accuracy of electronic storage and retrieval. Those of us who have been weaned on the cult of rote ought to realize that the object of our worship is not the content, but the values of a process. The act of memorization—the discipline and rigor required—shapes the individual, not the myriad facts being inscribed in the wrinkles of the brain. The argument that we are better human beings because of the agony of the process can be persuasive, but not convincing when we depend upon the results of data. The notion of a voluminous memory as a desirable human trait has been weakened as memory and knowledge are attenuated by the computer. The point is perhaps demonstrated by an example of our willingness to place our faith in the tradition of knowledge or the computer.

THE COMPUDOCTOR SAVES ALL

Someone in your family is acutely ill and requires the best medical care possible. In this hypothetical situation you will be required to choose between two types of individuals who will administer aid: an excellent physician, particularly diagnostically skilled, who treats you with the kindness and respect that the insecure patient often requires, and a less personable doctor, equipped not with a dazzling and reassuring personality, but with the latest computer—connected with every other relevant data bank in the world—to be used to diagnose the illness and prescribe both treatment and medication. What is your choice? Most probably, several factors will play a role in your decision: the seriousness of the illness, the possibility of curing it, and the degree of trust you have in either the traditional or the computer-assisted physician. The decision is painfully difficult to make and yet a surprisingly predictable one. Each of us could be persuaded to reverse our initial position. Most of us would prefer the old-fashioned reliable, kind, and wise doctor to the smooth computer-assisted technician—unless it could be demonstrated that the chances for recovery were good if the directives of the compudoctor were heeded, but uncertain if the warm wise personality tried to provide the cure. It's a gamble, and who among us would not pick the healing of the body over the soothing of the soul if the odds were high enough?

Perhaps you object to the apparent absurdity of this fantasized dilemma, but be assured that such choices will be commonplace. Dr. Jerrold S. Maxmen's account of future medicine, *The Post-Physician Era: Medicine in the 21st Century,*[20] delineates three alternative medical future scenarios. The first is the "Physician-Centered Model," which is the paradigm of current medical practice in the United States where the doctor makes diagnostic and treatment decisions. Although highly technical machines and computers might be used in the process, the doctor orchestrates and interprets the entire affair. The doctor is the all-powerful authority figure in whom we blindly place our trust. In the "Health-Team Model," paraprofessionals and allied health personnel are added, but the physician is still responsible for coordinating and supervising them. The "Medic-Computer Model" is a radical departure from the previous paradigms:

> Under this system computers would render most of the technical diagnostic and treatment decisions presently being made by physicians, while *medics,* a hitherto unknown type of health care professional, would pro-

vide the supportive and some of the technical tasks currently being performed by doctors. Because a medic-computer symbiosis would usurp all the tasks presently assigned to physicans, doctors would be rendered obsolete.[21]

The nuances of the medical future can be argued, but it is certain that radical changes will occur and have already begun. It is doubtful whether we the patients will have a say in the matter, although our attitudes and feelings ought to be crucial to our physical and mental health.

An editorial in *Nursing Outlook* presented a fictional conversation between two patients waiting at a Regional Computer Diagnostic Center in August 1991.

Kim: Here for a checkup?

Jesse: Sure I am.

Kim: You sound enthusiastic.

Jesse: Why not?

Kim: Come on, how could you possibly like having a computer do your physical exam?

Jesse: I do like it. In two minutes that machine is able to tell me everything I ever wanted to know about my body—and then some. If there is anything wrong, the printout will also give me all my treatment options. It's fast, and its really thorough.

Kim: And cold and indifferent.

Jesse: It won't pretend to assume responsibility for my health and well-being, if that's what you mean.

Kim: You're not afraid to make your choices based on the data in your print-out? How can you be so sure that the data are accurate? Don't you ever worry about computer error?

Jesse: Of course I do. But I think it's a lot less risky than it was in the days of the one-system specialist. As crazy as it may seem, I get more of a sense of my own wholeness this way. Besides, the specialists programming these computers are the best in their fields. It used to be so much harder to know what you were buying.

Kim: I feel a lot less sure of what I'm buying now. It's like being a slab of meat, lying on that table and having those probes go over me from head to foot. Alone. Just me and that clicking, blinking, buzzing machine. Chilling, really. I don't understand why we have to use every new piece of technology we have. Why do we complicate our lives so?

Jesse: You have the choice not to use it, but at least it's there if you want it. Remember what started to happen just before we moved into computer diagnosis?

Kim: What?

Jesse: I'm talking about maldistribution. Even in high-density areas with an abundance of physicians, the poor and the elderly were being turned away when they wanted to see a private physician. Washington had withdrawn enough support from the cost of medical care to make poor people unattractive patients for private practitioners; the elderly took a long time to examine. If physicians accepted people from these groups as patients, they couldn't make enough money. So they stopped accepting them.

Kim: So?

Jesse: Nothing. The computer doesn't discriminate. That's all.

Kim: Right. It makes the same mistakes on everybody. I'm getting out of here.[22]

The Quantification of a Profession

Our theme is not the quality and cost of contemporary medical care, but rather the linkage between knowledge and the computer and how it affects certain professions and our attitudes toward them. The new partnership requires the quantification of knowledge to transform it into a useful commodity. Focusing on the physician emphasizes the change because the relationship between patient and doctor is so intimate and often is formed under dramatic, potentially traumatic, circumstances. The medical relationship is based on the patient's assumption that the physician has particular qualifications and talents. The choice of physician is made by the patient's intuitive judgment that the doctor's medical training, experiences, and understanding qualify that person as someone who is an expert healer.

The conspicuous medical diplomas are not read, but are a part of a necessary created scientific ambience. Ideally, we are willing to trust another human being with our lives because we respect that person's knowledge and wisdom. It is a domain of expertise from which we are excluded because of a lack of training, skill, and credentials. We assume that this person has acquired enough knowledge and information that the proper decision will be made on our behalf.

Extraordinary scientific developments have enhanced and complicated contemporary health care. The physician practices and seeks to keep up to date with the explosion of medical data—an almost impossible task. The solution to part of the knowledge gap is to transfer that body of material to a microcomputer accessible to the average physician. No longer will the harried doctor require a magnifying glass to scour the drug catalogue for the correct potion. If however, the means and nature of knowledge acquisition change, so will the intimate relationship between practitioner and client—in any professional relationship. If the mystique of specialization, upon which our trust is based, is undermined, the perception of the professional changes. What happens to authority and power when it is transferred from the brain to the nimble fingers? The compudoctor might be an extraordinary physician, but that person, or rather our image of the person and role, has been transformed from that of a brilliant and wise diagnostician to that of a highly efficient and skillful technician. Whether that assessment is founded in fact is not as important as the effect the judgment has upon any subsequent interactions with members of the medical profession. The adoration of the physician, the placement of that person upon a professional and social pedestal, is irrevocably eliminated, for better or for worse, as our ideal of "doctor"—and all that is represented by that image—is forever changed.

The Professional

As a child everyone was asked the question more than once, "What do you want to be when you grow up?" As adults we interact with others on the bases of professions and hierarchy. Where do we place a particular profession on the scale of admiration and respect. What would you want your child to become if your dreams could be realized: an engineer, an astronaut, a pilot, a teacher, a chef, a plumber . . . ? Do we remunerate occupations in direct proportion to our perception of their importance? What makes a particular profession "special?" In *The Micro Millennium*, Christopher Evans suggests that the hierarchical position of a profession is tied to the degree to which that occupation is open or closed in terms of public knowledge.

The professions, as you might expect, guard their secrets closely, insisting on careful scrutiny and rigorous training. But this state of privilege can only persist as long as the special data and rules for its administration remain inaccessible to the general public.[23]

Since a profession's status is related to the discipline's monopoly of knowledge, the potential availability of data to anyone who cares to inspect the information threatens the monopoly and status of the profession. Whether the material will be understood or not is another matter. "Once the barriers which stand between the average person and this knowledge dissolve, the significance of the profession dwindles and the power and status of its members shrink."[24] The demystification of overblown professional ego is healthy, but the implications of the communication revolution far exceed the humbling of professionals. Evans observes that the impact of the new technology "will be greatest in those areas where high levels of skill and training are normally required and which, at one time, were assumed to be *the least* likely to succumb to automation."[25] A reversed social order in which those who practice such manual skills as carpentry, plumbing, and automechanics receive the approbation formerly reserved for highly educated specialists will mean some adjustments in personal interaction. The economic reversal seems to have begun if one judges value or worth on the basis of financial remuneration. The professionals who offer the services most needed by society receive the highest salaries. Whether economic value is an index of social value is another matter, but in all probability our estimation of a person is linked to economic status.

In the service industry dedicated to the support and maintenance of the computer-telecommunications system, programmers and information brokers assume the elite aura. Those who understand the interfacing of all the system's components are valued. Those who provide and control information are influential. Anyone who processes data or services the equipment within the system is absolutely required. An information bureacracy begins, and has begun, to evolve. The development of service structures is not news. Just reflect on our interaction with banking, government, and education institutions. What is new is our dependency on a knowledge and information service industry whose potential scope is incomprehensible. Imagine a switchboard through which any and all needed information will be routed and which interconnects any known institution and person with the data required at any time or place. The concept of the Information Utility makes the telephone company, once believed to rule us all, seem like an anti-quated exhibit in a communications museum.

THE INFORMATION BROKER

An information broker is a middle person or agency who provides information in the form of stored, computerized packages of data or documents to customers who have a need for information and are willing to pay for it. Companies and individuals whose primary function is to search, collect, and buy data in order to sell it to distributors which include that material in their offerings to home or business customers are "information brokers." They are absolutely vital to the system, since without the necessary content the "information utility" can not serve its function. The phenomenon of individuals and groups dedicated to gathering and distributing knowledge and information is not new. What is different at this time is that so few can be in control of so much. The harvester of information has usurped the position of the originator of knowledge. We have acknowledged both, but primarily now honor the former. The process of gathering knowledge, while honored, was subservient to that of original thinking. One served the other. But the rise of the "information broker" indicates a shift of priorities and a change of attitude toward knowledge and information. The "information broker" is a specialist bartering data; he is neither teacher nor student, but a salesman.

Andrew Garvin created "a supermarket of information" called FIND/SVP and wrote *How to Win With Information or Lose Without It* in which the philosophy behind the information business is explicated.

> What, exactly, is information? Dictionary definitions equate it with knowledge. But knowledge is the *result* of information. Information consists of facts, news, statistics, impressions—pieces of *intelligence* that singly or together increase your awareness. Rather than making assumptions that might lead to failure, make the assumption that the information needed for success is out there somewhere and available at a reasonable price. Then go look for it.
>
> The cost of anything is usually equated with the money needed to acquire it. But this is the consumer approach to cost. The business and professional approach equate cost to value. The value of information is equal to the *time* and *money* spent in acquiring it and the ultimate *profit* estimated from its use.[26]

The Business Development Manager of an information service firm articulated the following mission:

> We are an international information business service. Our product is information. Our product is providing the individual with the answers to questions . . . information to a marketing type of individual, financial planner, strategic corporate planner. It is the key to the decision making process. "Do we enter into a specific market? Do we have competitors in this field?" At times these individuals do not have the resources, nor the time, nor the insight. "Well, I have this question, where do I go to find the answer?" "I have this information need, where do I find the answers?"

Should students and scholars turn to information brokers for research purposes?

> We don't turn scholars away. We welcome all sorts of individuals. The problem comes with, "it's going to cost me all that money!" . . . I can make several recommendations for individuals to be most cost effective, to cut down research time. I often do that for individuals because I have an emotional attachment to information, to the information industry. I want to help people.

When asked if he would have any reservations permitting a Ph.d. candidate to use his services for research, our informant replied,

> I wouldn't look down upon the person. A lot of Ph.d. or Masters candidates may be involved in full-time jobs, they have two children to support, or they just do not have the time to go out there and do the research that is necessary. Undergraduates have come to us, even high school students have come to us to do their homework. "It will cost you some coin!" Some of the information brokers are one to two-man operations who go along the avenue of working with undergraduate students. They are not term-paper mills, they merely research the work at an hourly rate.

The Demotion of Wisdom

The new educational paradigm includes computer technology. The basic structure of the computer and its telecommunication connection has its roots in the ideal of the individual struggling to amass all there was to be known, because the human being was the primary repository of learning. Whether that model became outmoded because the task was too immense or we were inventive enough to relieve ourselves of that personal responsibility by creating and using extramental technology for the purpose, the traditional model became antiquated. The new technology is more efficient and more capable of dealing with the staggering amount of data required for twentieth century survival.

In a world where great stress is placed on the ability to find necessary data, and less emphasis is placed on the personal serendipitous retention of information itself, the middle person, the one who controls what information is available, grows in importance. When the stress is upon the accumulation, storage, and retrieval of data, the information broker is essential. The problem that arises is whether that merchant image is so powerful and compelling that it will influence the traditional marketers of wisdom whose stature was based upon our regard for the acquisition of knowledge. The most obvious figures that come to mind besides the physician are the lawyer, the judge, the priest, and the teacher, each of which has declined in stature over the past several decades. The status of each has been threatened by communication innovations which transfer the power to diagnose, judge, and interpret from the educated elite to the technically proficient.

In an environment where the information broker is a paramount figure, the practice of teaching begins to change to conform to a new and different pattern. In a radical departure from the traditional view of teacher as sage, the teacher has come to be regarded as a medium of information. Is the teacher seen as a thought provoker whose main function is to stir, stimulate, and goad the student into awareness and understanding? Or is the teacher seen as a purveyor of facts whose mind is to be sucked dry of all that is relevant so that the student can use it for specific purposes? The alternatives are not quite as dramatic as portrayed here, but the contrast is helpful to make the point. The "binary model" of education transfers the on-off mentality of the computer (you either know or do not know) to the human scholar-student interaction. We are beginning to evaluate teaching with the standards of the efficiency of an electronic machine which is far more capable, in most instances, of retrieving needed data than the human being. The demise of human frailty and inefficiency is not to be celebrated lightly. To reject the extraordinary potential of the computer-telecommunications complex because it is new and because it threatens some traditional notions we have about the nature of knowledge acquisition would be a grave mistake. In all probability we have little choice as we are increasingly forced into daily interaction with the information utility. But we do have the capability and option of understanding the implications of a phenomenon that transforms our attitudes toward knowledge and information—and perhaps of utilizing the new technological innovations to enhance traditional values.

If knowledge is power, the powerful are those few who control or monopolize that commodity. If access to knowledge is potentially equally distributable to all those who have the desire and need for it, than knowledge is divorced from power, because the monopoly is dissolved. In that sense, the information utility equalizes the distribution of information and portends some radical social shifts. When product and efficiency are emphasized, having access to and effectively manipulating data are necessary skills to be admired and rewarded. There is no contest between the brain and the small powerful microprocesser: the criteria of utility favors the infallible and efficient electromechanical device. The dilemma is apparent. The efficiency of the computer makes possible the availability of information to all, but overshadows the quality of wisdom which is acquired out of a passion for understanding and connection. It is not helpful to divide the wise from the facile, to deplore the inefficiency of knowledge or to extol the practicality of a binary mentality. The challenge of the future is to preserve the sanctity and excitement of knowledge while harnessing that spirit of inquiry to the technical support of computer technology. The symmetry of the contemporary sage requires both the capacity to access data and the ability to think. It is such a duality of which W. H. Auden speaks:

> Those who will not reason
> Perish in the act:
> Those who will not act
> Perish for that reason.

Eight

The Limits of Community

I'm friendly with the people on the block. When you're outside in the summer working, you can sit around and talk to them, but they're not the friends we visit back and forth. When we moved in we were the youngest couple on the block. They were all a lot older than we were. We really had no common interest. Now, the people who have moved in are a lot younger than I am, so I'm not going to socialize with the people on the block, but you can be very friendly with them. I see them all the time.

I don't think you generally tend to be buddy buddy with neighbors. I think that most of the community would prefer not to be. If you ever had a fight with a buddy who lived next door, you've got to live with him. It's the old New England saying, strong fences make good neighbors. I think a lot of people really believe that. I really have no interest in socializing with the people. I want to be friendly with them, but they are not the people I'll play golf with, I'm not going to a dance with, or stop and have a drink with them, but there's plenty of people that I do.

Interview with a Neighbor

So this is hell. I'd never have believed it. You remember all we were told about the torture-chambers, the fire and brimstone, the "burning marl." Old wives tales! There is no need for red-hot pokers. Hell is——other people!   Jean-Paul Sartre, No Exit

The applicability of "community" to life in the twilight of the twentieth century is complex. Each of us is touched by "community" because no one can live without it. Yet there is little agreement over what is meant by the term, perhaps because the acceptance of a particular definition suggests a social perspective that implies not only a style of living, but also responsibility and obligation to others.

The definitions cover a broad range of facets.

1. a social group of any size whose members reside in a specific locality, share government, and have a common cultural and historical heritage. 2. a social group sharing common characteristics or interests and perceived or perceiving itself as distinct in some respect from the larger society within which it exists (usually prec. by *the*): *the business community; the community of scholars.* 3. *Eccles.* a group of men and women leading a common life according to a rule. 4. *ecol.* an assemblage of plant and animal populations occupying a given area. 5. joint possession, enjoyment, liability, etc.: *community of property.* 6. similar character; agreement; identity: *community of interests.* 7. the community, the public; society: *We must consider the needs of the community.*[1]

"Community" suggests the romantic idea that there was once an idyllic world in which a "special" relationship between the individual and other human beings existed, in an environment that was peaceful, harmonious, and hospitable. This mythic notion contrasts the present with the past, pits urban against rural existence, and compares the technological present with a less complicated and more primitive environment. "Community" has been idealized and elevated until, "like motherhood and apple pie, it is considered synonymous with virtue and desirability."[2] This fantasy of the better life induces a strange ritualistic choreography in which sophisticated urbanites flee to the rural hinterlands to escape the menace of the city—only to rush back fearing that some sort of pastoral rigor mortis might set in. This ritual is not limited to the United States. In the preface to his description of a French village, *Village in the Vaucluse,* Laurence Wylie describes witnessing a similar romantic obsession as "city dwellers escape to the country as frequently and for as long as possible. Their dream is often to re-create what they assume the old communal life must have been."[3] Wylie observes that French city planners have been aware of this phe-nomenon and have attempted to "adapt what they see as the secret of village happiness to modern needs."[4] Whether it is possible to convert the village ambience to an urban environment is questionable, but more to the point is Wylie's observation that "although rural life has lost its place in the French economy, the public commitment to the myth it nurtured is stronger today than ever before."[5]

The belief that life is better in the easy-going atmosphere of the "pure" countryside ignores the lure of big-city life. The search for the "ideal" pastoral setting is not necessarily to be interpreted as a rejec-tion of contemporary urban surroundings. "The good old days" are symbolically attractive but pragmatically less compelling. Historically, the same ambivalence and confusion have always been expressed in comparisons of the "good old uncomplicated days" with contemporary social turmoil.

GEMEINSCHAFT TO GESELLSCHAFT

A number of theorists have examined the nature of community and the effects of industrialization upon the individual's relationship to place. The sociologist Ferdinand Tonnies distinguished in his native Germany between "community" and "society." Tonnies called the former *Gemeinschaft*—an organization in which the constituents were bound together through tradition, friendship, and kinship. It describes a com-munity bound together by reciprocal sentiment. Tonnies called the community bound together by contract, division of labor, and fluctuat-ing dynamic relationships a *Gesellschaft*. His bias toward *Gemeinschaft* is clear, but as Richard Sennett points out in *The Fall of Public Man,* Ton-nies "regretted the loss of *Gemeinschaft* but believed only a 'Social Ro-mantic' could ever believe it would ever appear again."[6] Ferdinand Tonnies stated:

> All intimate, private, and exclusive living together, so we discover, is understood as life in *Gemeinschaft* (community). *Gesellschaft* (society) is public life—it is the world itself. In *Gemeinschaft* with one's family, one

lives from birth on, bound to it in weal and woe. One goes into *Gesell-schaft* as one goes into a strange country.[7]

Gemeinschaft is place-oriented because the relationships stem from contact and the intimate knowledge that individuals have of each other and their cooperation in "labor, order, and management."[8] The *Gemeinschaft* is an organization of social relationships which is preindustrial and whose model is the family with its obligations, responsibilities, and attitudes. Tradition, respect, ritual, deep bonds, and commitment characterize this construct.

The industrial revolution introduced urban life, specialization, and a more complex societal organization than had existed. The shift from an agrarian to an industrial base requires the development of new services, different employment needs, and the relocation of workers into new patterns of housing.

> *Gesellschaft,* an aggregate by convention and laws of nature, is to be understood as a multitude of nature and artificial individuals, the wills, and spheres of whom are in many relations with and to one another, and remain nevertheless independent of one another and devoid of mutual familiar relationships.[9]

The intimacy of *Gemeinschaft,* the bond of that closely knit community, is weakened as the individuals of an industrial society become less concerned with mutual obligation, but more involved with personal gain and self growth. Ultimately the person no longer identifies with or feels affinities with others located in the same living-working-playing space, because that space has been redefined. Individuals who interact with each other because of contractual ties instead of social commitment become a collection of psychologically isolated individuals.

> In the *Gesellschaft,* as contrasted with the *Gemeinschaft,* we find no actions that can be derived from an a priori and necessarily existing unity; no actions, therefore, which manifest the will and the spirit of the unity even if performed by the individual; no actions which, in so far as they are performed by the individual, take place on behalf of those united with him. In the *Gesellschaft* such actions do not exist. On the contrary, here everybody is by himself and isolated, and there exists a condition of tension against all others.[10]

This portrait of life in an industrialized society is somewhat dismal and pessimistic, but it is also overdrawn in its polarization of positive and

negative attributes. Nevertheless, the theoretical construct is most helpful in shedding light on the persistence of community as an important
and supposedly cherished value.

The Community of Place

Community is generally linked with territory. Community as place can
refer to a street, a neighborhood, a village, even a town. It is a sense
of identity that members share. The sense of awareness has been described by Franklin Giddings and Joseph Gusfield as their "consciousness of kind." The appeal to act as a member of the community, to
give special consideration to fellow members, and to place their aims
above those of others and one's own must presuppose a recognition of
the reality of the community and of the member's affiliation to it. The
"consciousness of kind" thus depends on perceiving that there is such
a kind and that one is part of it.[11]

"Consciousness of non-kind," as a corollary to a "consciousness of
kind," requires the collective identity which crystallizes community. It
is dependent upon the awareness that some people or groups are excluded from "our community." The "outsiders which threaten the
community, help to define it." Robert Redfield in *The Little Community*
lists four qualities which characterize this sense of place: distinctiveness,
smallness, homogeneity, and self-sufficiency.[12]

Redfield's "little community" belongs to a less urbanized world, one
that is more rural than most of the areas where the Western world's
population lives. What is, however, noteworthy is that in a world moving away from the agrarian structure of the village and into the complex structures of the technologically based urban-surburban *Gesellschaft,*
the romantic notion of the community-oriented village predominates as
a model of a better existence. Even though the urban dweller would,
most likely, reject life in the little community because of its claustro-
phobic atmosphere and demands, values of the past persist, affecting
our present attitudes. Ronald Blythe, writing about the English village,
elaborates on this paradox of values in which the past influences the
present so strongly.

> The townsman envies the villager his certainties and, in Britain, has
> always regarded urban life as just a temporary necessity. One day he
> will find a cottage on the green and "real values." To accommodate the
> almost religious intensity of the regard for rural life in this country, and

to placate the sense of guilt which so many people feel about not living on a village pattern, the post-war new towns have attempted to incorporate both city and village—with, on the whole, disheartening results.[13]

Ghettos, Neighborhoods, and Community

The economic factors which stimulated the growth of cities and the urban-suburban complex also were fundamental in forming specific communities structured and based upon ethnicity and race. The Greeks, the Jews, the Chinese, the Irish, the Puerto Ricans, the Blacks, the Poles, *et al.* lived and live in communities or ghettos (ghettos are communities seen from the perspective of those living in restrictive pockets of poverty) probably because there were excluded or limited to specific areas and because they needed each other. And need is a paramount requisite for community. The city represented (and to some extent, still does) a place where opportunity for economic advancement existed, where dreams could become a reality, a place from which to begin. For people living in relative splendor outside the ghetto, these communities were convenient areas to put the different, perhaps undesirable, although curiously necessary members of society. For those outside, these communities became interesting curiosity places to visit: stimulating and exciting areas where one could find restaurants to suit each and every palate, meet strange cultures of different and infinite style, and discover freedom from the restrictions imposed by one's own obligations.

In *The Urban Wilderness: A History of the American City,* Sam Warner, Jr. lists three traditional goals by which cities can be judged: competition, community, and innovation.[14] Competition refers to the equal and fair opportunity provided to each citizen for economic survival and ease. Community, according to Warner, "holds that a successful city should encompass a safe, healthy, decent environment in which every man participates as a citizen, regardless of personal wealth or poverty, success, failure."[15] Innovation involves the opportunity for expression within a free and open environment, that the "variety and individual of citizens should find expression in new ideas, new art, new tools and products, new manners and morals."[16]

The blessings and the lure of "the big city" are, however, mixed with less favorable aspects of living. The quality of urban life is very much influenced by the fact that so many people are crowded into a relatively small area and a great many of them have to move in and out of the center area every day. The need for office space, living space, and transportation for millions of closely confined people results in congestion, frustration, and the opportunity for crime. As the cities grew during an extraordinary acceleration of technological development, the patterns of interaction between its inhabitants was radically altered. Communication, which is absolutely vital to community, was transformed by two developments: efficient means of transportation and rapid modes of communication. With the advent of streetcars, buses, railways, subways, and automobiles, and the media of telephone, telegraph, newspaper, radio, television, and the computer, the interaction that had occurred in public places began to be dispersed.

Going Outside to Be Alone

Sitting on the front steps to gossip and pass the time of day was an urban social interaction that has almost become obsolete. "Hanging out" on the corner represented more than a way to relieve boredom, for it involved the exchange of ideas and the opportunity for sociability. But "stoop-sitting," in neighborhoods with handy front steps set close to the sidewalk, and its counterparts were never really built into the fabric of American society. They were often restricted to the ethnic pockets of cities or tolerated in suburbia under the scrutiny of the local police. European public social intercourse stands in contrast. The Italian piazza, the French café, the English pub, the Spanish plaza, and the Greek taverna are still central to the dynamics and structure of those societies. Perhaps one explanation for the different approach to public interaction is the American historical preoccupation with space and territory rather than with the interaction induced by proximity. The art of public relationships has never been quite as important to Americans as it was in some other cultures. This is what Marshall McLuhan was referring to when he said that "North Americans may well be the only people in the world who go outside to be alone and inside to be social."[17] This is not to deprecate the sociability of Americans, but merely to suggest that it takes another form. An American uses his or her home to entertain with great élan and style, while the European invites guests into his or her home only on special occasions and is social in public. The European ventures out to be seen, while the

American assumes the cloak of invisibility while outside the home. The desire for social anonymity is part of the American psyche, and the lack of privacy, the public display without choice, forced upon the younger inhabitants of small villages or rural areas drives many of them away to the "city."

Nevertheless, there was a time in the United States when public interaction was essential to both economic and social development, a time when the panaroma of the streets revealed the character of the society.

> It is the urban street that from the first origins of settlements has acted as the principal place of public contact and public passage, a place of exchange of ideas, goods, and services, a place of play and fight, of carnival and funeral, of protest and celebration. Its place in the web of associations that have sustained human society is therefore paramount.[18]

But the importance and role of the street as a social phenomenon changed as the automobile redefined and emphasized the street as thoroughfare, as it transformed the arena of transaction into a hostile environment that pedestrians seek to traverse and drivers must navigate. The causes of such change are complex and multiple, but clearly the technology of transportation and communication were and are very much involved in the transformation.

> Whereas the extensions of man's linguistic powers (transcription and transmission) now function chiefly without demanding his presence in the artifact street, the extensions of his locomotive power (transportation) have, in urban contexts, taken place chiefly by superimposing themselves on the streets. Thus, while the street is still a necessary place of movement from one part of the city to another, it is possible to converse with a neighbor, to receive news from down the street or from far away, to be entertained, or, if predictions are correct, to be able to shop without leaving one's home.[19]

The possibility for insularity and isolation are increased when the opportunity for public interaction is decreased and the need and demand for community is altered. The antitheses of the former values of community become prized in an urban-suburban environment as attitudes change. For some, privacy replaced loneliness. Detachment and impersonality become emblematic of freedom, while for others they indicate psychological isolation and alienation. Although freedom from community attachments and pressures can be a luxury, it is paid for by an existence of relative nondependence. The obligations of consanguinity may yet endure, but they cannot be assumed or demanded from others who inhabit the same relative living space. Are you obliged to your neighbor?

Scholar and essayist Joseph Epstein asks the question, "What, really, is wanted from a neighborhood?"

> Convenience, certainly; an absence of major aggravation, to be sure. But perhaps most of all, ideally, what is wanted is a comfortable background, a breathing space of intermission between the intensities of private life and the calculations of public life. In the neighborhood, relationships need not become entangled, behavior need not be triggered by motive. In the neighborhood—between the drama of the household and the battlefield of the career—the casual reigns, the quotidian dominates. In the neighborhood, life mercifully flows on.[20]

The comment reveals a relationship with community that is less intimate, more detached, but strangely demanding. This new neighborhood is a neutral environment which serves as a kind of amniotic fluid in which the organism is sheltered, perhaps even nurtured, but under the best of circumstances seldom disturbed, never really in contact with others. Nevertheless, while the demands have changed, community is still important, and Epstein cries out against the homogenization of neighborhoods as they are "boutiqued" in the tide of urban renewal. Certainly, the old neighborhood vanishes, even that "comfortable background" begins to fade, as the gentrification of community eradicates the spirit that mobilizes and provides its substance.

The Neighborhood and the Telephone

It's strange that amid all this change the plaintive cry for community still persists. No doubt, the frantic pace of urban life and the rate of technological acceleration have changed the concept of community, but the qualities and values represented continue to symbolically influence daily relationships. Milton Mayer has written a thoughtful essay on the subject of community, delineating the dilemma of yearning for the qualities and values of community in a world where they appear to be unattainable because they have become outmoded, old-fashioned relics of a previous time. In "Community, Anyone"[21] Mayer reveals a quandary he found himself in during the Vietnam War when he contemplated withholding payment of the tax on his telephone bill as a protest against the war; it had been rumored that such funds were slated toward military appropriations. He decided, however, to pay the tax because the danger of being penalized by having the telephone removed was too threatening a punishment. "I can live without my principles. I cannot live without my telephone. My telephone enables me to live *without community*"[22] [my italics].

> I live in a farming "community," five miles or so from the busy college town in, or beyond, which (some of them ten to twenty miles beyond) my friends and colleagues live. My nearest neighbor could not hear me holler if I needed help. But I don't need to holler for help—not as long as I have my telephone. My friends and colleagues are in the same case. We rarely need each other, but we want each other now and again, and the telephone (and the car appended to it) meet our want. This kind of community we have and it does very nicely; we need neither hang together nor hang separately.[23]

There was a time when the true confirmation of one's existence was finding one's name, address, and telephone number inscribed in the local telephone directory. At that point, one knew that one belonged. While the telephone remains a primary utility without which one becomes a social eccentric, our attitudes toward the telephone directory and belonging have changed radically, particularly with the rise of the fashionable "unlisted telephone number."

Telephone companies provided two conditions for anonymity: "not listed" and "not published." "Not listed" (a service not provided by all companies) simply means that the number is not listed in the directory but is available upon request. "Not published" means that the number is not listed in the directory and also is not available to the operator. In the case of an emergency, the call would be routed to a supervisor who had access to the number and who would judge whether it merited being connected.

The reasons for requesting an unpublished number are summarized by a telephone company spokesperson as the "six p's": paranoia, privacy, prestige, professionalism, pomposity, and poverty. The urge is strong enough that an estimated 13 percent of this nation's phone population is willing to pay the one-time conversation fee and the monthly charge in order not to appear in the telephone directory, to remain telephonically incognito. Estimates of this trend are that in some urban areas the percentage of "non-published" telephone numbers runs from

20 to 35 percent. Choosing not to be included in the telephone directory is symbolic of a nonpublic attitude—a statement that privacy is paramount. Mr. Mayer needs his telephone, but not his neighbor. He, like many others, has chosen relative remoteness and electronic connection and is thereby "freed from involuntary membership in the nonvoluntary community."[24] The obligations of community have been abrogated by the media of community. Mayer states that "the technological cornucopia of my time has broken the bonds—or the bondage—of community. The new forces are centrifugal. They have snapped all the vestigial (or embryonic) synapses of community."[25]

In his lament Mayer wonders whether there is "any basis for supposing that the anti-communitarian process is reversible, any basis for supposing that it won't continue to accelerate."[26] And he answers his own question in the negative while dreaming and yearning for those former times when community was not merely a sentimental dream, but a reality one did not have the option of rejecting. It isn't that community has merely faded into the background, or that it has evaporated while the human being gropes for that mysterious element of territorial cohesiveness that is suddenly missing. The loss of the need for community is the result of numerous technological and social factors, but our tacit approval is generally not acknowledged or noticed as we dream of better days. The pragmatic aspects of communal place have been *rejected*, while the value is bronzed and enshrined.

> We are told that man is a rational animal and a political animal. I would like to suggest that he is also a wistful animal. Wistfully he dreams of community and of really belonging to a community. Wistfully he wishes that he had need of his neighbors. Wistfully he wishes that his neighbors needed him.[27]

THE MEDIA COMMUNITY

Community is rooted in face-to-face dialogue between two or more people in the same place to air problems, issues, and concerns of mutual interest. It is, however, quite apparent that contemporary dialogue is not restricted to *a* place since the media of communication have dispersed or expanded the possibilities through the "reallocation" of space. Traditionally, dyadic relationships, except those extended in time through written correspondence, were physically manifested at a specific point in time and place. The contract was signed in a specific office, the meeting occurred at a café, the discussion was accompanied by several pints of ale. In contrast, a telephonic relationship exists by connecting two places in time. The concept of place and our relationship to it requires reassessment because of the impact of the electronic media. The spectator watches the football or baseball game, or any other event, without being at the site where it occurs. Our perception of an event and the place where it is held are no longer contiguous. Stated differently, communication is no longer restricted by place; community is being redefined by the media of communication.

Melvin N. Webber elaborates upon the recognition of media's impact in his discussion of "community without propinquity" or "non-place communities." [28] Webber asserts that spatial proximity is not a necessary condition of community and that the urban realm is "neither urban settlement nor territory, but heterogeneous groups of people communicating with each other's space." [29] The absence of spatial propinquity, the actual physical nearness of individuals, is less important to the maintenance of social communities today because modern media have eliminated "cohabitation of a territorial place" as a prerequisite for community.

> With few exceptions, the adult American is increasingly able to maintain selected contacts with others on an interest basis, over increasingly great distances; and he is thus a member of an increasing number of interest-communities that are not territorially defined. [30]

In the contemporary urban/suburban world most people are potential members of a series of "non-place" communities. Such multiple membership in non-place communities constitutes a person's "media community." Such communities do not require the simultaneous physical presence of its members since they are connected by print and electronic media.

Membership in a media community is not the same as mere exposure. Watching a particular television program or listening to the radio to be entertained or to find out the latest news is making contact with the available and shared media. It does not necessarily suggest a relationship with another human being, nor does it signal identification and association with a group. But the decision of the jogger to subscribe to a magazine dedicated to the world of running indicates affiliation and identification. The scholar's publication in journals dedicated to an academic discipline and research methodology is association without propinquity. The computer freak's participation in long-distance improvisational fictional communities or communication with unseen friends involves an electronic commitment.

Webber describes a hierarchical continuum in which the more professionally oriented individuals have a higher proportion of their time invested in the media community than others. The higher one is on the socio-economic scale, the greater the proportion of time spent in "non-face-to-face interaction" through channels such as the telephone, telegraph, audio and video recordings, professional journals, written correspondence, computer connections, and books. The intellectual elite, the specialized professionals (Webber refers to them as "cosmopolites"), are part of communities which transcend space restrictions.

> They share a particular body of values; their roles are defined by the organized structures of their groups; they undoubtedly have a sense of belonging to the groups; and by the nature of the alliances, all share in a community of interests. Thus, these groups exhibit all the characteristics that we attribute to communities—except physical propinquity.[31]

On the other hand, Webber indicates that members of the working class rely much more on "limited 'close-knit networks' of social relations."[32]

Media Environments and Media Community

Each person lives in an identifiable place distinguished from all other sites. The answer to "where do you live?" must locate your dwelling in a meaningful geographical context, and it is determined by your perception of who asks the question. To someone from the Bronx the New Yorker identifies himself as coming from Manhattan. To the Texan the Manhattanite labels himself a New Yorker. To the Greek in Athens the New Yorker represents himself as an American. No one can be from nowhere. Whether that place can be called a community is another matter, but it is a "home" which has a geographical context and, depending on the media services that are available, a specific "media environment." Some of the media are intrinsic, originating in the specific environment, and some extrinsic, or imported into the area.

Radio and television stations, while mandated by the Federal Communication Commission to serve the community's "public interest, convenience, and necessity," serve a much larger constituency than a well-defined community, because of economic necessity. In the New York area, WCBS-TV, WCBS-AM and FM cover a portion of three states and serve over seventeen million people. Both legal and natural boundaries are erased by the electronic media. There was a time when the physical community and the media environment were essentially synonymous or congruent, when the newspaper served and defined a relatively small area. Although today most mass media identify themselves as representing and serving a particular community, the population in such areas must be large enough to economically support the media. *The Chicago Sun, The New York Daily News, The Bangor News,* WCIX in Miami, WVUE in New Orleans, KLBJ-AM in Austin, WBBM in Chicago—all cast a broad defining shadow over their dominions. But one medium does not constitute the "media environment," rather that environment is composed of all media that are *potentially* accessible to the inhabitants of a geographical area, thereby providing a common pool of mediated experience.

The allocation of radio and television stations by the FCC was based upon the distribution of signals which would not interfere with each other and which would provide the nation with a blanket of coverage. Fewer television stations were assignable because the signal of each required a wider bandwidth of the electromagnetic spectrum than radio stations. In order to establish simultaneous national distribution of programs, networks were established through the connection of stations located in specific areas of the country. The structure of radio and television broadcasting *was* inexorably tied to geographical entities. The legislation was quite clear in tying a broadcasting license to a community.

> What we propose is documented program submissions prepared as the result of assiduous planning and consultation covering two main areas: first a canvass of the listenting public who will receive the signal and who constitute a definite public interest figure; second, consultation with leaders in community life—public officials, educators, religious, the entertainment media, agriculture, business, labor, professional and eleemosynary organizations, and others who bespeak the interests which make up the community.[33]

Community service became the criterion for evaluating broadcast stations when, because of the scarcity of channels that could be located on the electromagnetic spectrum, the federal government began to regulate broadcasting systems. This traditional configuration of radio and television dissemination is now radically changing because of the development of alternative means of dissemination, particularly home video cassettes, cable television, satellite transmission, and low-power television stations.

The video cassette system shifts the control of dissemination directly into the hands of the audience who can rent or buy films for home viewing and can tape off the air any programs they deem worth recording; whether the viewer is at home or not is not important, since recorders can be pre-set. As of 1985 some 20 million video cassette recorders had been sold, and the sale and rental of tapes comes close to two billion dollars annually. The implications of this major development are important, particularly in regard to public interaction. The demise of the neighborhood motion picture theatre is well on its way. With the VCR, crowds are avoided, lines are unnecessary, and the cost per viewing is far less than the price of a ticket. The film experience is becoming a private affair.

Cable television, which began as a means of providing television signals to communities in which reception was poor or nonexistent, has developed into a multimillion dollar business which not only facilitates transmission, but increases the number of channels available to each location. The number of channels is theoretically unlimited since the signal travels by wire rather than by air waves. Systems with 40, 50, and 60 channels are now commonplace. As of 1985 there were nearly 6000 cable systems in the United States serving 83 million subscribers (approximately 40% of all TV households). Therefore, the regulation of television channels because of their scarcity is no longer a viable basis for the administration of the medium.

Satellites provide an additional means of disseminating electronic signals on an almost global scale. Through dishes which provide the links to the satellite, any local program can be transformed into a national or an international event. This capability, in connection with cable transmission, makes the concept of "local" television stations serving their immediate areas technologically obsolete. "Superstations" such as TBS in Atlanta, WOR in New York, and WGN in Chicago are examples of program dissemination systems in which the signal's site of origination is irrelevant.

An increasing number of people, apartment complexes, and communities are purchasing their own satellite dishes. *Channels* estimated that at the beginning of 1985, 600,000 dishes had been purchased by individual home owners; the magazine forecast a monthly sale of 60,000 new dishes.[34]

> Pointed toward any of the more than 20 North American communication satellites, a backyard "satellite earth station" can intercept not only all the regular television channels, but also the "raw feeds"—not intended for public viewing—sent by broadcast and cable networks to local stations and cable systems across the country. With an unobstructed view of the southern sky, it can receive 75 to 100 television channels and retransmission of 40 FM radio stations.
>
> The dish collects the satellite's faint microwave signal and amplifies it 500,000 to one million times. A cable carries the signal indoors to a "downconverter," which changes the frequency to one that can be received by an ordinary TV set. The apparatus often has a remote-control device that lets the viewer redirect the motorized dish toward another satellite and select one of its 24 channels.[35]

One dramatic example of communities acquiring dishes is a number of small towns in Canada which have pooled their financial resources to create illegal rebroadcasting systems. The municipalities are installing large-dish antennas which are tuned to receive and relay to the wired subscribers, signals from American satellites. Such an act violates Canadian law and international treaties existing between Canada and the United States. The firms that install the dish antennas are thriving since it is not illegal to build and install the necessary structure, but it is illegal to turn on the system and to "pirate" the television signals. The Canadian government's efforts to intervene and close down the operations have met with strong resistance. A spokesperson for one such installation in Chetwynd, British Columbia, said "I wouldn't want to be the official that came into Chetwynd and pulled the plug. You could only do it if you had a jail big enough for the whole town, because everybody contributed."[36] In the town of Geraldton in Northern Ontario the mayor has threatened to deputize all the town's inhabitants in order to prevent any seizure of the illegal dish by federal authorities. The desire for entertainment in remote areas is a strong incentive to break the law. The drama and irony of the situation are of the first order. A small town reaps the treasure of a satellite that hangs 22,500 miles above it, and the threat of not being allowed to continue this twentieth-century media piracy results in unity and a temporary sense of community.

All of these technological developments de-emphasize the connection of "person" and "community." One exception to this trend are the low-powered television stations approved by the Federal Communication Association several years ago. Such stations operate with limited power, covering only a range of from 10 to 20 miles, and are designed to serve the needs of specific communities in ways that the traditional high-powered station cannot.

> Low-powered enthusiasts envision the stations serving small, sometimes discrete, audiences whose needs are ignored by large commercial stations and even by public stations: local community debates over zoning rules, high school sports, and news of particular interest to black, Hispanic, and other ethnic communities. Many small communities with no station of their own could for the first time get programs of local interest, instead of relying on the distant signal of the big-city stations.[37]

To what degree such stations will succeed is, at this time, questionable. At the end of the 1984, 260 low-powered stations were on the air, but three-quarters of them were in Alaska.[38] Their potential to become economically viable is highly doubtful, since their cost is higher than originally thought.

Another exception to the de-localization of media services are the "public access" and "local origination" stations which were at first mandated by the FCC in the establishment of cable franchises, but which have, for the most part, been ineffective, noncompetitive, and unappealing in contrast with the numerous other programming sources provided by cable.

The Myth of the Third Wave

Technological media innovations give each person access to the world without the need for physical proximity. Ironically, as the home becomes the center of each person's universe from which radiate the antennae of involvement with the world, contact with one's immediate community is lost. Video cassette recorders, personal computers, electronic mail, videotex, the telephone, radio, and satellite dishes alter how and with whom human beings interact. It is this new communication configuration that Alvin Toffler describes in *The Third Wave,* in which he prophesies the emergence of the "electric cottage" and a "return to cottage industry on a new, higher, electronic basis, and with it a new emphasis on the home as the center of society."[39] Toffler's provocative thesis is based on several concurrent trends. One of these is that Western society is shifting the proportions of its labor force as electronics revolutionize manufacturing. Fewer blue collar workers are required to perform jobs that previously required many. On the other hand, the electronification of manufacturing requires more and more white collar workers. The shift in work force allocations not only redistributes people into work roles as the priorities of society change, but it also redefines where they work. In the same way that the place where we live has and is being transformed by our greater reliance upon the media of communication, the place where we work is affected. Indeed, the concept of *"the* work *place,"* as distinct from *"the place* where we live" or *"the places* we play" becomes ambiguous because *"the place"*—a specific and separate territory where work is performed—is not required for all forms of production. The technology of work is being shifted into the home, not for all professions, but certainly for many. The addition of the computer console, the facsimile machine, tele-conferencing equipment, and the "smart" correcting typewriters provide the necessary paraphernalia for the accomplishment of many tasks, if not most, tied formerly to *"the office place."* Why does a secretary *have* to be in physical proximity to the boss to perform his or her duties? What white collar professions *require* the physical presence of coworkers assembled in a specific location called an office if they can be electronically interconnected? When is interpersonal contact between white-collar professional and client *necessitated?* The stockbrocker does not have to see the investor. The banker need never meet the depositor. The travel agent never sees the airline respresentative and hardly ever needs to see the traveller. When must an editor come into contact with an author?

Toffler's view of the future is supported by the argument that rising energy costs will stimulate the move into the electronic cottage. He poses the following question: "When will the cost of installing and operating telecommunication equipment fall below the present cost of commuting?"[40] He predicts that such a point is imminent and that the "telecommuter" will help alleviate the transportation crisis.

Toffler's optimistic analysis of the impact of technology upon community is intriguing, particularly as he maintains that the electronic cottage will be a major part of a "home-centered" society. It is his believe that electronic connection will result in greater family stability since there will be fewer traumatic shifts as a result of professional relocation. Rather than a new job requiring a move to another site, the employee can, according to Toffler, "simply plug into a different computer."[41] With more permanent relationships greater community participation and identification would result.

> The electronic cottage could help restore a sense of community belonging, and touch off a renaissance among voluntary organizations like churches, women's groups, lodges, clubs, athletic and youth organizations. The electronic cottage could mean more of what sociologists with their love of German jargon, call *Gemeinschaft*.[42]

Toffler acknowledges a common public reaction toward computers and telecommunications, the fear that they "will deprive us of face-to-face contact and make human relations more vicarious,"[43] but he considers these reactions "naive and simplistic."[44] He claims the reverse, that the technology will facilitate relationships in some cases and liberate individuals from the traditional tyrannies of the urban-suburban cycle, thereby freeing them to participate in a true community.

What Mr. Toffler confuses is connection with allegiance. While the web of electronic connection will continue to be woven by the telecommunication infrastructure of the industralized world, and it is quite certain that fewer extraterritorial excursions into the outside world will be necessary, it is improbable that a group of isolated persons who incidentally are found in the same location should relate to each other. Incidental proximity of living quarters does not create a neighborhood or induce community, not without the need and opportunity that acts as a catalyst for cohesion and solidarity.

As more and more people gain the world through the central electronics of the living room, the ambience of the outside environment becomes less and less important. Relationships with neighbors are tolerated, but certainly not preferred, when connections of choice can be mandated with fingertip digital control. We coexist in a locale and share a media environment which has expanded far beyond our physical environment. At the same time, each of us lives in a series of media communities which do not exist as geographical entities. These communities are defined, served, and created by the media of communication that a scattered membership selects. Without intentional participation and identification the media community cannot exist.

THE IMPERFECTION OF THE PERFECT WORLD

The new mode of living will not be confined to the home. People will stroll outside, shop, talk, contemplate the grass, take the sun, and even go to work, but the focus will be inward. It is an existence of scope and freedom without the inhibiting restrictions imposed by non-negotiable obligations. In contemporary life each individual attempts to control the number and type of associations and contacts. It is a welcome relief from the tyranny of place where choice is a luxury instead of an inalienable right. And yet, something indefinable is missing in everyday life. It is hard to pinpoint what is wrong, because possibly there is nothing wrong. One has a gnawing feeling, however, that one's space is not quite in synchrony with that of other inhabitants of the same space. Everyone marches to the sound of their own drummer and any sense of fitting into the melange of the urban cacophony fails. The signs of imperfection in the perfect world are innocuous. Perhaps it is suddenly being aware that you and your neighbor do not greet each other as you pass in the hall. Or is it the realization that when you are in trouble you don't ask the person next door but rather call your friend on the other side of town? Could it be that the doctor's practice is around the block, but that he lives in another area and never remembers your name when you visit the office?

There are several indications that the absence of *Gemeinschaft,* a lack of obligatory connection with a community of propinquity, has left some sort of void not met by family or by media connections: the degree of mindless and passive media interaction in which we engage, the increasing need for mental health agencies and services to alleviate malaise, and the rise of media forms dedicated to therapy.

Any addiction is dysfunctional, and extended habitual television viewing is debilitating. Switching on the television set upon entering the house is an automatic reflex for many people. When the average television set is turned on for five and a half hours per day, selective viewing is at a minimum and one can assume that other daily activities have become restricted. Television as a repetitive ritual replaces social interaction with solitary activity.

Over the past several decades there has been a rising demand for mental health services, particularly counseling and therapy. State, county and private agencies provide psychiatrists, psychologists, and therapists to those in search of help. In addition, the increasing number of consciousness raising, encounter, support, widow, assertiveness training, mediation, and sexuality groups is nothing short of phenomenal. Small groups of individuals guided by a trained leader (who is paid for his or her services) meet weekly to discuss the problems that plague their daily lives. In a sense, these are therapeutic communities in which the participants interact in order to reveal, empathize, and discover how to cope with the intricacies of life. Therapy has always existed in some shape or form, although it might not have been labeled and recognized as a separate and distinct human activity. The institutionalization of the process and the elevation of therapy to a special niche suggests a response to a social system that is not providing the means of public introspection in the natural course of events.

All human beings experience periodic depression, emotional barriers, disappointments. All require the love and understanding of others who listen and perhaps respond with encouragement and words of advice. That need often cannot be satisfied by immediate family members, no matter how close. The opportunity for supportive interaction is built into the structure of a community of place. But in the urban environment, as the community of places recede and is replaced by media community, as the church and the synagogue lose their functional identity, as public areas for social intercourse such as pubs, cafés, and piazzas are rediscovered and become the playgrounds of nouveau-riche America, the natural and necessary cathartic interaction between two or more concerned persons takes place instead in a therapeutic community dedicated only to that specialized task.

The correlation between income level and membership in media communities has its counterpart in mental health care. While those in the upper income brackets do not have a monopoly on neuroses, they do have, one would assume, a more formalized and sanctioned social structure of therapeutic consultation. Generally, the therapist functions outside a community of place and is relegated to a relatively neutral venue in an atmosphere controlled by time and fee.

The fee can be avoided and the emergency or problems can be confronted if one turns to the newest therapeutic community—the media therapist.

Q: I want to ask you a question. Is there anything wrong with not masturbating? I mean if you don't have the urge?

A: Absolutely nothing wrong. How old are you?

Q: I'm 19.

A: Absolutely nothing wrong, and when you will fall in love and find
     the right person, the sexual urge is going to be developing and
     you're going to have a good sexual life . . .
     Hello, you're on the air.

Q: One night I was with my girl friend in the house I had two
     orgasms. We went down to the car where I proceeded to have
     four more orgasms.

A: Okay, Hold it! Hold it! Let me tell you something.

Q: That's not it yet.

A: Wait! wait! wait! Let me tell you something right way, because I
     can't even answer that. The only thing I can tell you, you happen
     to be a very lucky guy, all right?

Q: So just enjoy it?

A: Just enjoy it is right. See, you knew already what I'm going to say.
     Have a good time. Bye-bye.[45]

Dr. Ruth Westheimer provides sexual advice and entertainment on
both radio and television to those who are willing to make a telephone
call and allow their conversation to be heard by all those listening to
the station. If you can't afford the cost of therapy, turn on the radio
and experience the public agony of others. The radio psychologist has
become an important addition to the radio station's cast of personae
along with the weatherperson, critic, and news team.

   There are several variations of media therapy: public, including phone-
in radio and television programs and a long tradition of syndicated
columns such as "Dear Abbey," and private media therapy, which primarily connects individuals by telephone to someone with responsive
skill. There are numerous crisis line organizations which provide aid
and comfort to potential suicides, battered wives, alcoholics, etc. Phone
sex, facilitated by the multifunctional credit card, connects the sexually
deprived person with someone who fulfills sexual fantasies until satisfaction is reached. And then there is "computer sex."

   Our main goal is titillating entertainment. Imagine participating in an
   electronic free-for-all, or having an intimate one-on-one fling with someone
   who shares your personal needs and desires. Or picture yourself asking
   a well known x-rated film star for a sexual favor! *all from the privacy and
   comfort of your own home* [author's italics]. If you've been frustrated by

other national online services' attempts to stifle your sexual freedom, the answer has arrived.

The mediation of the therapeutic community indicates a curious paradox as deep seated emotional needs are answered by a system in which the response is available, but detached and depersonalized.

From the beginning of time the human spirit has dreamed of transcending the restrictions of time and place, of escaping from the confines of the physical. The ideal was and still is to faithfully communicate the thoughts of one person to another who would be able to understand. Never before has that ideal been so close to attainment. The scope of communication is now virtually unlimited as global contact has become a norm rather than an extraordinary event. The media of communication have freed us to reach beyond the physical limits imposed by the body and interact without the restraints of propinquity.

But the excitement of discovery also creates problems as our obligations to others are altered. To gain global community and lose commitment to those around us is a serious issue. It is clear that the relationship of self to family, neighbors, and friends is being redefined. Priorities and values need to be examined. What is loneliness in a world where the choice of media contact with another person is always possible? Where do obligations toward one's neighbor end and where do the duties toward a media community begin?

NINE

A Hare and a Tortoise

What a dull heavy creature (says a hare) is this same tortoise! And yet (says the tortoise) I'll run with you for a wager. "Twas done and done, and the fox, by consent, was to be judge. They started together, and the tortoise kept jogging on still, 'till he came to the end of the course. The hare lay'd himself down about midway and took a nap; for, says he, I can fetch up the tortoise when I please: but he over-slept himself it seems, for when he cam to wake, though he scudded away as fast as 'twas possible, the tortoise got the post before him, and won the wager.

Aesop according to Sir Roger L'Estrange

A STITCH IN TIME

One interpretation of "A Hare and a Tortoise" is that those who endure, persevere, and continue to patiently struggle are eventually rewarded with success. The implication is clear, that the tedium of persistence overcomes energetic but erratic effort. The key commodity is time, which must pass, which heals, endures, accelerates as one ages, and decelerates with impatience. Everything takes time and time is to be respected. Those who survive its vagaries reap the spoils of remuneration and acclamation.

And yet time has always stirred the imagination of human beings. The compelling urge has been to transcend the restrictions imposed by always having to be in one place at any one particular time. In an artistic vision we have journeyed into the past, traveled into the future, stopped aging, grown quickly, been instantly transported from one place on earth to another—or to another planet or dimension, returned from the dead, heard the voices of those long gone, and given life to inanimate objects.

In the non-fictional world, technological innovations have harnessed time by preserving images, permitted humans to fly from one spot to another faster than the speed of sound, experimented in rejuvenation and cryogenics, made possible the moving of the human voice and image around the earth, allowed performers to talk, act, and sing long after their demise, and made possible the repetition and duplication of any event.

We celebrate the virtue of the tortoise but secretly wish the hare had won. Certainly it was not the case of the better creature having won, because the hare was defeated only by his arrogance, not his lack of ability. Swiftness, which should have decided the race, was overshadowed by the more traditional and dependable virtues—persistence and diligence. The fable celebrates persistence as a virtue, while swiftness is somewhat tainted with negative characteristics.

Given a duo with fairly equal sets of personality traits, whom would you root for in the race, the slowest contestant? The answer is clear, that there is little intrinsic value in being slow, except when that trait is associated with patience. Completeness, thoroughness, meticulousness et al. are linked with patience and endurance; a slow pace, virtue, and permanence are antithetical to speed.

It is this type of conflict which occurs when the new media technologies collide with traditional values. Each of the essays in this volume in some way concern a conflict in time. "The Talking Tombstone" seeks to demonstrate how values in general are being altered by innovations in media technology. It asks how the value of perpetuity and attitudes toward death might be affected by the possibility of preserving one's "persona" though a living audio-visual computerized legacy. The issue of preservation is raised somewhat differently in "The Fake Horses of San Marco," which looks at the implications of the aesthetic object as product, which can be duplicated, replicated, and "transmitted" to the consumer. In "Walls of Sounds" I consider the substitution of an acoustical world of one's choice for one's actual surroundings, or aural time and place. "The Ambiguity of Perfection" analyzes how a blurring of reality occurs as the use of audio and videotape confounds the distinction between past and present and television reality becomes the basis of our comprehension of the world.

Was it ever possible to know everything? The sages of the past stoically strove for an end they knew they could not reach. "The Last Person Who Knew Everything" explores the effects of the computer on the acquisition and value of knowledge. Who would have predicted that *instant* knowledge could be achieved and that a machine would allow humans to know as much as is needed in as little time as possible and with the least intellectual exertion necessary. Once, "The Limits of Community" were dictated by the time it took to physically leave the community—to be out of touch. Media technology has dissolved those limits by electronically connecting almost any two people anywhere in the urbanized world. Instead of communities of place, the electronic revolution has created electronically connected media communities.

"The Telltale Tape" discusses the impact of the instant replay, an accurate record of an athletic moment, on winning and sportsmanship. The television viewer is entertained by a second look at a play, while the referees continue to make instant judgments. The modern telephone and its assorted electronic equipment provides instant connection, without revealing the user's identity. It is a communication instrument which allows for anonymity although its function is most certainly social. "Talking to Someone Who Isn't There" explores so-called sexual intimacy over the phone. In the "Perception of Perfection" the use of sound technology to create "the perfect musical performance" is analyzed. How does the fragmentation and rearrangement of performances in the recording studio affect our standards?

Values are not immutable. They are responsive to the dynamics of history and experience. And because they are relative and debatable, they persist and sometimes coexist with and are challenged by conflicting values. Such states of tension exist whenever major social change occurs. The effect, for example, of Gutenberg's invention of movable type in the fifteenth century upon the entire civilized world was extraordinary. Every major technological innovation in communication modifies the value systems of subsequent generations.

When values are in flux, contradictory beliefs often coexist within the same individual—one espoused, the other practiced. Community versus privacy, sportsmanship versus winning, instant gratification versus persistence, ease versus effort, uniqueness versus replication, are guiding but contradictory companions. Is it possible to violate the rules of sportsmanship or to applaud the violators of sports ethics without a twinge of guilt? Can one celebrate privacy and abstain from responsibility to one's neighbor without a pang of regret? Is long-acquired wisdom to be compared with instant electronic access to information without a sense that the results were not legitimately earned?

It is necessary to re-evaluate the attitudes and values which guide social perceptions and interactions. The alternative is to adopt a series of double-sided values in which one half is a platitude and the other a belief based upon pragmatism. Traditional values are being rocked and tested at an accelerating pace. It is dismaying to suddenly awake to the realization that one's beliefs are passé, that one is isolated in a dynamic system of change in which cherished beliefs have become old-fashioned vestiges of the past.

A FABLE REVISITED

What a dull heavy creature (says a hare) is this same tortoise! And yet (says the tortoise) I'll run with you for a wager. 'Twas done and done, and the fox, by consent, was to be the judge. They started together, and the tortoise kept jogging on still, till he came to the end of the course. The hare stopped about midway and telephoned several business colleagues to establish a business meeting after he crossed the finishing line. I can fetch up the tortoise when I please as long as I keep track of the time. I think I have just enough time to write several letters on my portable computer (and he did). The wrist alarm rang and he scudded away as fast as 'twas possible because there was a race and a wager to be won. The tortoise got to the post just a moment after he did and so the efficient hare won the wager.

No matter what anyone says, the values of the past steadfastly maintain that perseverance will be rewarded and that haste makes waste—despite the evidence to the contrary, that the swift reap the rewards!

Notes

INTRODUCTION

1. Russell Baker, "Ringing Up The Past," *The New York Times,* October 4, 1981, p. 17.
2. "Inventors," *People,* November 7, 1977, p. 39.
3. Victor Huge, *The Hunchback of Notre Dame.*
4. Julian Marias, *Generations: A Historical Method* (University, Alabama: The University of Alabama Press, 1970), p. 11.
5. Melvin L. DeFleur, William V. D'Antonio, and Lois B. DeFleur, *Sociology: Human Society* (Glenview, Illinois: Scott Foresman and Company, 1976), p. 127.
6. Milton Rokeach, *The Nature of Human Values* (New York: The Free Press, 1973), p. 25.

CHAPTER ONE

1. Walter Benjamin, "The Work of Art in the Age of Mechanical Reproduction," reprinted in *Film Theory and Criticism,* edited by Gerald Mast and Marshall Cohen (New York: Oxford University Press, 1974), p. 613.
2. *Ibid.*
3. *The New York Times,* November 16, 1980, p. 47.

4. *Ibid.*

5. Amei Wallach, "The Trouble With Prints," *Artnews,* May 1981, p. 62.

6. Wallach, p. 63.

7. Benjamin, p. 615.

8. Benjamin, p. 616.

9. Michael J. Arlen, *Thirty Seconds* (New York: Penguin Books, 1980), p. 47.

10. Horace Newcomb, *TV: The Most Popular Art* (New York: Anchor Books, 1974), p. 22.

11. *Ibid.*

12. Henry Pleasants, *Serious Music—And All That Jazz* (New York: Simon and Schuster, 1969), p. 41.

13. Dwight MacDonald, "A Theory of Mass Culture," in *Mass Culture: The Popular Arts in America,* edited by Bernard Rosenberg and David Manning White (Glencoe, Illinois: The Fress Press, 1957).

14. Alan Gowands, *The Unchanging Arts: New Forms for the Traditional Functions of Art in Society* (New York: J. B. Lippincott, 1971), p. 18.

15. Barbara W. Tuchman, "The Decline of Quality," *The New York Times Magazine,* November 2, 1980, p. 38.

16. Tuchman, p. 39.

17. Tuchman, p. 40.

18. Gilbert Seldes, *The Great Audience* (New York: Viking Press, 1950), p. 264.

19. Seldes, p. 257.

20. Umberto Eco, *A Theory of Semiotics* (Bloomington: Indiana Press), p. 181.

21. Richard E. Stone, "Antico and the Development of Bronze Casting in Italy at the End of the Quattrocento," *Metropolitan Museum Journal,* vol. 16, 1982.

CHAPTER TWO

1. John J. O'Connor, *The New York Times,* January 3, 1982, section 1, p. 1.

2. Herbert Zettl, *Sights, Sound, Motion: Applied Media Aesthetics* (Belmont, California: Wadsworth Publishing Company, 1973), p. 254.

3. Zettl, p. 255.

4. Benedict Nightingale, " 'What If a Mars Landing Were Faked,' Asks Peter Hyams," *The New York Times,* May 28, 1978, section 2, p. 11.

5. Douglas R. Hofstadter, *Godel, Escher, Bach: An Eternal Golden Braid* (New York: Basic Books, Inc., 1979), p. 10.

6. Hofstadter, p. 15.

7. Peter Funt, "Television News: Seeing Isn't Believing," *Saturday Review,* November 1980, p. 32.

8. Jack Nelson, "Stockman's Statements Roil Capital," *Los Angeles Times,* November 1, 1981, p. 1.

9. Howard Rosenberg, " '60 Minutes' Ambushes '60 Minutes,' " *Los Angeles Times,* September 28, 1981, section VI, p. 8.

CHAPTER THREE

1. Alan Wurtzel, *Television Production* (New York: McGraw-Hill, 1979), p. 363.
2. *The New York Times,* October 12, 1980, section 5, p. 4.
3. Joe Fall, "Instant Replay No Way to Settle Close Call," *The Sporting News,* January 26, 1980, p. 7.
4. Larry Felser, "Refs Need TV Help, Not Lame Excuses," *The Sporting News,* January 26, 1980, p. 25.
5. *Ibid.*
6. Bud Greenspan, *We Wuz Robbed* (New York: Grosset and Dunlap, 1976), p. 188.
7. Glenn Sheeley, "Instant Replay Faces Instant Death," *Pittsburgh Press,* March 16, 1979, p. C-8.
8. Greenspan, pp. 188–189.
9. Greenspan, p. 190.
10. John Richard Betts, *America's Sporting Heritage: 1850–1950* (Reading, Massachusetts: Addison-Wesley, 1974), p. 186.
11. Robert H. Boyle, *Sports: Mirror of American Life* (Boston: Little, Brown, and Co., 1963), p. 241.
12. *Ibid.*
13. Betts, p. 113.
14. *Webster's Sports Dictionary* (Springfield, Mass: G & C Merriam, 1976), p. 415.
15. *The Oxford English Dictionary* (Oxford: Clarendon Press, 1933), p. 669.
16. *Ibid.*
17. *The Oxford Universal Dictionary of Historical Principles* (Oxford: Clarendon Press, 1955), p. 1980.
18. Howard S. Slusher, *Man, Sports, and Existence: A Critical Analysis* (Philadelphia: Lea and Febiger, 1967), p. 147.
19. *Ibid.*
20. Slusher, p. 148.
21. *Ibid.*
22. Lawrence Rosenfield, Laurie Hayes, and Thomas Frenz, *The Communicative Experience* (Boston: Allyn and Bacon, Inc., 1976), p. 31.
23. Lawrence et al., p. 36.
24. Lawrence et al., p. 40.
25. *Ibid.*
26. Geunther Lueschen, "Cheating in Sports," in *Social Problems in Athletics: Essays in the Sociology of Sport,* edited by Daniel M. Landers (Urbana: University of Illinois Press, 1976), p. 67.
27. Lueschen, pp. 73–74.
28. Dick Young, "Young Ideas," *New York Post,* May 17, 1982, p. 56.

CHAPTER FOUR

1. Russell Baker, "What a Crazy Statement," *The New York Times,* July 5, 1980, p. 19.

2. Local Law No. 57, Noise Control Code, The City of New York. Published by the City Record.

3. *Ibid.*

4. "Police Confiscating Radios Blared in Public," *The New York Times,* June 30, 1980, p. B7.

5. *Ibid.*

6. *The New York Times,* October 5, 1980, p. 49.

7. R. Murray Schafer, *The Tuning of the World: Toward a Theory of Soundscape Design* (Philadelphia: University of Pennsylvania Press, 1980), p. 77.

8. Edward T. Hall, *The Silent Language* (New York: Anchor Books, 1959), p. 162.

9. Edward O. Wilson, *Sociobiology: The New Synthesis* (Cambridge, Mass: Belknap Press, 1957), p. 257.

10. Wilson, p. 257.

11. Hall, p. 182.

12. *Ibid.*

13. Wilson, pp. 261–62.

14. Schafer, p. 33.

15. *Ibid.*

16. Schafer, p. 214.

17. Dr. Joyce Brothers, *High Fidelity Trade News,* March 1982, p. 13.

18. Richard Warren, *The Chicago Sun Times,* January 25, 1980.

19. Hans Fantel, *The New York Times,* July 7, 1980.

20. *Ibid.*

21. Ron Alexander, *The New York Times,* July 7, 1980, p. B12.

22. *Roller Skating,* October 1980, vol. 2, no. 5, p. 17.

23. Brothers, p. 13.

24. Acoustiguide tape "Monet Unveiled," Museum of Fine Arts, Boston.

25. Interview with Ed Woodard, Acoustiguide Corporation.

26. *Ibid.*

27. Interview with William Warner, Vice President of Marketing, MUZAK.

28. *Ibid.*

29. "Acoustical Privacy in the Open-Plan Office—Updated," *Architectural Record,* June 1978, p. 141.

30. MUZAK brochure.

CHAPTER FIVE

1. Henry Pleasants, *Serious Music—And All That Jazz!* (New York: Simon and Schuster, 1969), p. 91.

2. Interview with Immanual Wilheim, Department of Music History and Literature, Hart College.

3. Century of Sound (Montreal: Studio Artistique Un Deux Trois Limitée, 1977), p. 30.

4. *Ibid.*
5. Charles Repka, "Digital Records: Rolls Royce or Edsel?" *Keynote,* June 1980, p. 17.
6. *Ibid.*
7. Interview with Gordon Titcomb.
8. *Ibid.*
9. Artur Schnabel, *My Life and Music* (New York: St. Martin's Press, 1961), p. 96.
10. Liner Notes, "From Every Stage," JCB Productions (released 1976).
11. Ed Woodard, "Where Am I and What's Going On Here?: Plausibility As Determinant of the Locus of Perception," Unpublished paper.
12. *Ibid.*
13. *Ibid.*
14. Interview with Joan Peyser, former editor of *Musical Quarterly.*
15. Joseph Horowitz, "The Trouble with Recordings: A Polemic," part I, *Keynote* (October 1980).
16. Interview with Morton Gould.
17. *Ibid.*
18. Horowitz, p. 22.
19. *Ibid.*
20. Horowitz, p. 19.
21. Interview with Wilheim.
22. Interview with Gould.
23. Interview with Titcomb.
24. Walter Kerr, "A Theater Critic Gets that 'Synchin' Feeling," *New York Times,* December 4, 1977, section II, p. 1.
25. Brochure, IRCAM, Centre Georges Pompidou, Paris.
26. *Ibid.*
27. Interview with David Wessell, Head of Pedagogy, IRCAM.
28. Gary Karr, "The Ice Age Returneth," *Music Journal,* December 1973, pp. 22, 35.

CHAPTER SIX

1. "Bell Labs President Says Society Will Benefit from New Telecommunications Technology," Bell Labs press release, November 28, 1979.
2. *Ibid.*
3. "Technology for Universal Service of the Future," *Background Papers on Science and Technology,* Bell Labs press release, undated, p. 5.
4. "Technologies in the Eighties," A Multi-Media Address by Albert E. Spencer, Executive Director, Business Project Planning, Bell Labs.
5. *New York Magazine,* July 30, 1984, p. 90.
6. David K. Berlo, *The Process of Communication: An Introduction to Theory and Practice,* (New York: Holt Rinehart and Winston, 1960), p. 106.

7. *Ibid.*
8. Warren Weaver, "The Mathematics of Communication," in *Communication and Culture,* edited by Alfred G. Smith (New York: Holt, Rinehart and Winston, 1966), p. 15.
9. Bell Labs press release, October 6, 1980.
10. *Ibid.,* p. 54.
11. *The Random House Dictionary of the English Language* (New York: Random House: 1966).
12. Phillip Howard, *New Words for Old* (New York: Oxford University Press, 1977), p. 53.
13. *Ibid.*
14. Ronald Abler, "The Telephone and the Evolution of the American Metropolitan System," in *The Social Impact of the Telephone,* edited by Ithiel DeSola Pool (Cambridge, Mass.: MIT Press, 1977), p. 318.
15. *Ibid.*
16. Advertising for "Phone Songs."
17. Interview with Hugh Gigante, Periphonics Corporation.

CHAPTER SEVEN
1. Walter J. Ong, S. J. *Knowledge and the Future of Man: An International Symposium* (New York: Holt, Rinehart, and Winston, 1969), p. 3.
2. *The New York Times,* July 19, 1981, p. 29.
3. Russell Baker, "Terminal Education," *The New York Times Magazine,* November 9, 1980, p. 29.
4. *Ibid.*
5. Eric A. Havelock, *Preface to Plato* (Cambridge, Mass.: Belknap Press, 1963), p. viii.
6. Harold A. Innis, *The Bias of Communication* (Toronto: University of Toronto Press, 1951) p. 33.
7. Ong, pp. 5.
8. Ong, pp. 5–6.
9. Gilbert Highet, *Man's Unconquerable Mind* (New York: Columbia University Press, 1954), p. 66.
10. *Ibid.*
11. *Ibid.*
12. Bertrand Russell, *Human Knowledge: Its Scope and Limits* (New York: Simon and Schuster, 1948), p. 421.
13. *The Random House Dictionary of the English Language* (New York: Random House, 1966).
14. *Ibid.*
15. Kevin Robins and Frank Webster, "Information As a Social Relation," *Intermedia,* vol. 8, no. 4, July 1980, p. 30.
16. Program for the *Information Utilities '81* conference.

17. *Ibid.*
18. Anthony Smith, *The Geopolitics of Information: How Western Culture Dominates the World* (New York: Oxford University Press, 1980).
19. *Ibid,* p. 111.
20. Jerrold S. Maxmen, *The Post-Physician Era: Medicine in the 21st Century* (New York: John Wiley & Sons, 1976).
21. Maxmen, pp. 6–7.
22. Penny A. McCarthy, "Magnetic Bubbles," *Nursing Outlook,* August 1981, p. 459.
23. Christopher Evans, *The Micro Millennium* (New York: Viking, 1979), p. 111.
24. Evans, pp. 111–112.
25. *Ibid.*
26. Andrew P. Garvin and Hubert Bermont, *How to Win With Information or Lose Without It* (Washington, D.C.: Bermont Books, 1980), p. 19–21.

CHAPTER EIGHT

1. *The Random House Dictionary of the English Language* (New York: Random House, 1966).
2. Marcia Polly Effrat, *The Community: Approaches and Applications* (New York: The Free Press, 1974), p. 2.
3. Laurence Wylie, *Village in the Vaucluse* (Cambridge, Mass.: Harvard University Press, 1974), p. v.
4. *Ibid.*
5. *Ibid.*
6. Richard Sennett, *The Fall of Public Man* (New York: Alfred A. Knopf, 1977), p. 221.
7. Ferdinand Tonnies, *Community and Society,* translated and edited by Charles P. Loomis (New York: Harper Torchbooks, 1963), pp. 33–34.
8. *Ibid.*
9. Tonnies, p. 76.
10. Tonnies, p. 65.
11. Joseph R. Gusfield, *Community: A Critical Response* (New York: Harper and Row, 1975), p. 34.
12. Robert Redfield, *The Little Community and Peasant, Society, and Culture* (Chicago: University of Chicago Press, 1961), p. 4.
13. Ronald Blythe, *Glendfield: Portrait of an English Village* (New York: Pantheon Books, 1969), p. 16.
14. Sam Bass Warner, Jr., *The Urban Wilderness: A History of the American City* (New York: Harper and Row, 1972), p. 4.
15. *Ibid.*
16. *Ibid.*
17. Marshall McLuhan, "Inside on the Outside, or the Spaced-Out American, *Journal of Communication,* vol. 8, no. 4., Autumn 1976, p. 46.

18. Thomas B. Czarnowski, "The Street as a Communication Artifact," in *On Streets,* edited by Stanford Anderson (Cambridge, Mass.: MIT Press, 1978), p. 207.
19. Czarnowski, p. 209.
20. Joseph Epstein, *Familiar Territory: Observations on American Life* (New York: Oxford University Press, 1979), p. 49.
21. Milton Mayer, "Community, Anyone?," *The Center Magazine,* vol. VIII, no. 5, September/October 1975, pp. 2–6.
22. Mayer, p. 2.
23. *Ibid.*
24. Mayer, p. 3.
25. Mayer, p. 4.
26. *Ibid.*
27. Mayer, p. 5.
28. Melvin M. Webber, and Carolyn C. Webber, "Culture, Territoriality and the Elastic Mile," *Taming Megalopolis,* edited by H. Wentforth Eldredge, vol. I, *What Is and What Could Be* (New York: Anchor Books, 1967), p. 38.
29. Melvin M. Webber, "The Urban Place and the Nonplace Urban Realm," *Explorations Into Urban Structure* (Philadelphia: University of Pennsylvania Press, 1964), p. 116.
30. Webber, p. 111.
31. Webber, pp. 109–110.
32. Webber and Webber, p. 40.
33. 25 Fed. Reg. 7291 (1960).
34. Richard Barbieri, "Backyard Dishes: Helping Themselves to Everything in Sight, *Channels of Communication,* vol. 4, no. 4, Nov./Dec. 1984, p. 64.
35. *Ibid.*
36. Blaik Kirby, "Firms Thriving on Sales of Dishes to Pirate TV," *The Globe and Mail,* Monday, May 26, 1980, p. 9.
37. Ernest Holsendolph, "Here Comes Low-Power TV," *The New York Times,* April 11, 1982, p. 6.
38. Michael Couzens, "LPTV: Long Climb in Low Gear," *Channels of Communication,* vol. 4, no. 4, Nov./Dec. 1984, p. 30.
39. Alvin Toffler, *The Third Wave* (New York: William Morrow, 1980), p. 210.
40. Toffler, p. 217.
41. Toffler, p. 220.
42. Toffler, p. 220–21.
43. *Ibid.*
44. *Ibid.*
45. "You're On The Air," *The SOHO News,* February 9, 1982, p. 14.

Index